W9-AQE-731

# David Garrick


## Twayne's English Authors Series

Herbert Sussman, Editor

*Northeastern University*

TEAS 403

DAVID GARRICK
(1717–1779)
*Reproduced from the painting*
*by Robert Edge Pine*

# David Garrick

## By Phyllis T. Dircks

*C.W. Post College*
*Long Island University*

*Twayne Publishers • Boston*

CARNEGIE LIBRARY
LIVINGSTONE COLLEGE
SALISBURY, N. C. 28144

*David Garrick*

Phyllis T. Dircks

Copyright © 1985 by G. K. Hall & Company
All Rights Reserved
Published by Twayne Publishers
A Division of G. K. Hall & Company
70 Lincoln Street
Boston, Massachusetts 02111

Book Production by Marne B. Sultz

Book Design by Barbara Anderson

Printed on permanent/durable acid-free
paper and bound in the United States of
America.

**Library of Congress Cataloging in
Publication Data**

Dircks, Phyllis T.
  David Garrick.

  (Twayne's English authors series; TEAS 403)
  Bibliography: p. 143
  Includes index.
    1. Garrick, David, 1717–1779—
Criticism and interpretation.
I. Title.  II. Series.
PR3469.D56  1985      822'.6      84–15818
ISBN 0-8057-6893-9

822.6
G241

*For Dick*

117418

# Contents

# About the Author

Phyllis T. Dircks, who holds her M.A. from Brown University and her Ph.D. from New York University, serves as consultant to the National Endowment for the Humanities and editor of the *American Society for Theatre Research Newsletter*. Professor Dircks has contributed numerous articles on drama to scholarly journals, including *The Shakespeare Quarterly, Theatre Notebook, Research Studies, Theatre Survey, Restoration and Eighteenth Century Theatre Research,* and *Studies in Burke and His Time,* and has written the Introduction to Kane O'Hara's *Midas: an English Burletta* for the Augustan Reprint Society. She has conducted and participated in meetings of scholarly associations including the Modern Language Association, the International Congress of the Enlightenment, the American Society for Eighteenth Century Studies, and the American Musicological Society. Fellowships have been awarded Professor Dircks by the American Council of Learned Societies, the National Woodrow Wilson Foundation, and the Danforth Foundation.

# Preface

Although David Garrick was recognized as a significant and successful playwright by his contemporaries, his substantial accomplishments in playwriting have been eclipsed for later generations by his stunning reputation as a brilliant actor. Although a number of his plays were performed into the nineteenth century, copies of the texts were often inaccessible, so that his work was not easily available for systematic study. The literary public, then, seduced by the entertaining and anecdotal biographies of Garrick written by two of his theatrical colleagues, Arthur Murphy (*The Life of David Garrick,* London, 1801) and Thomas Davies (*Memoirs of the Life of David Garrick,* London, 1808), as well as by the interesting accounts of some nineteenth-century devotees of the actor, has perceived him, almost exclusively, as the finest actor of his day.

But recognition of Garrick's indisputable excellence as an actor should not overshadow, but rather lead us closer to an appreciation of his playwriting talents. For Garrick's practices as a playwright were shaped by his experiences as an actor. This study examines those practices in Garrick's original plays and in his adaptations, considering his aims, examining his techniques, and appraising his success; it is the first study to examine the whole of Garrick's dramatic work. The study seeks to place David Garrick within the context of the eighteenth-century London on which he made an indelible imprint.

I acknowledge, with warm thanks, the assistance of the Research Committee of C. W. Post College of Long Island University, whose support aided my research into this fascinating subject.

Phyllis T. Dircks

*C. W. Post College*
*Long Island University*

# Chronology

1771  *The Institution of the Garter* at Drury Lane, October 28.

1772  *The Irish Widow* at Drury Lane, October 23.

1772  Alteration of *Hamlet* at Drury Lane, December 18.

1773  *A Christmas Tale* at Drury Lane, December 23.

1774  *The Meeting of the Company* at Drury Lane, September 17.

1775  *Bon Ton* at Drury Lane, March 18.

1775  *The Theatrical Candidates* at Drury Lane, September 23.

1775  *May Day* at Drury Lane, October 28.

1776  Final performance on stage, June 10.

1779  Dies in London, January 20.

1779  Buried in Poets' Corner, Westminster Abbey, February 1.

## Chapter One
# The Making of a Playwright

David Garrick, in his multiple roles of playwright, theatrical manager, and occasional poet, occupied a central position in the pulsating literary and theatrical world of eighteenth-century London. During a professional life that spanned thirty-six years, he made a significant impact on an ever-growing reading audience which bought numerous copies of the forty-seven plays he either wrote or adapted for the stage of the Theatre Royal at Drury Lane. That influence extended to the playhouse audience, which clamorously paid up to five shillings to see him perform in a wide variety of roles, ranging from the tragic portrayal of a heartbroken, repentant Lear or an anxiety-crazed, demoniac Richard III to a comic rendition of the quick-witted, able, lying valet in his own play of that name. His ninety-six roles were executed with such artistry that he was universally acclaimed the greatest actor of his day.

From 1747 to 1776, during his twenty-nine years as manager of the Theatre Royal at Drury Lane, one of the two patent theaters in London, he wielded inestimable professional power and had the ability either to promote or devastate the careers of playwrights and aspiring actors, actresses, musicians, and dancers. For good reasons, they regarded him as a formidable personality.

Happily, Garrick dispensed his varying responsibilities in the three areas of playwriting, acting, and managing with enviable efficiency, as he organized his professional life around his conception of theater as an elevating force in the life of a civilized society.

## The Lichfield Years

Garrick's view of theater emanated largely from the values he acquired during his youth at Lichfield and was later clarified and refined by the practical exigencies of day-to-day theatrical activities, which he engaged in from young manhood. Lichfield, a cathedral and garrison town of about three thousand inhabitants, located more than one hundred miles from London, offered young David Garrick a background of refinement and culture. He was the third of seven children born to Peter Garrick, an army officer stationed there, and Arabella Clough, daughter of a vicar in the Lichfield Cathedral. Born on February 19, 1717, young David fell heir to a rich and abundant social life which centered about the officers and their families, who were, for the most part, people of leisure and cultivation. Moreover, he was the beneficiary of a stimulating intellectual and cultural life because of his mother's close association with the Cathedral, the center of all intellectual activities in the town.

Garrick's father was known as "an honest valuable man,"[1] and the Garricks were recognized as one of the leading families. Years later Boswell confirmed this, noting that Samuel Johnson, another resident of the town, enjoyed "a kind reception in the best families at Lichfield. Among these I can mention Mr. Howard, Dr. Swinfen, Mr. Simpson, Mr. Levett, Captain Garrick. . . ."[2]

A precocious youngster, David benefited from yet another Lichfield association: that with Gilbert Walmesley, Registrar of the Ecclesiastical Court and resident of the Bishop's Palace. Walmesley, a learned, kindly gentleman who did not marry until the age of sixty, expressed an almost paternal affection for David. A friend of Captain Garrick, he allowed the young boy to range freely in his extensive library and later furthered his close relationship with Samuel Johnson. When David proposed leaving Lichfield for London in 1737, Walmesley provided him with a letter of introduction to his friend, the Reverend Mr. John Colson, calling young Garrick "as ingenious and promising a young man as ever I knew."[3]

Despite the social prestige afforded an army officer's family, the Garricks were not wealthy, and David's contact with genteel poverty marred his otherwise fortunate upbringing. Johnson describes the family as one "whose study was to make fourpence do as much as others made fourpence half-penny."[4] Though in a prestigious regiment, Captain Garrick spent thirty years of his service on half-pay, a common occurrence, due to the excess of army officers at that time. Garrick never forgot those years, and, though generous in his maturity, his spending of money was always cautious and analytic.

Years after leaving Lichfield for London in 1737 in the company of Johnson, Garrick maintained warm ties with Johnson and Walmesley, as he did with other Lichfield friends, particularly the prominent clergymen, Joseph Smith and Thomas Newton. Smith and Newton gave Garrick early and fulsome encouragement when, in the face of unflagging opposition from his family, he proposed to make a full-time commitment to the life of the theater.

Entrance into the theatrical world came naturally to Garrick, who had come into its milieu as salesman for the wholesale wine business that he had established in London with his elder brother, Peter. He frequently traveled to the theater district, visiting coffeehouses and taverns and meeting some of the players. After forming a fast friendship with Henry Giffard, a theatrical entrepreneur, and meeting the rising actor, Charles Macklin, Garrick soon discovered that the wine trade held no interest for him, compared with the fascination the world of theater exerted upon him.

## Garrick the Theatrical Personality

**The Playwright.** Garrick's formal entrance into the theatrical world occurred in a spectacular debut in which he played Richard III at Goodman's Fields, an unlicensed theater outside London. His stunning success in that role attracted the attention of all London and led to his playing a series of important parts. His direction was clearly determined.

Even before his appearance on stage, however, Garrick had identified himself as a playwright. *Lethe,* his first play, was a comic episodic sketch within a mythological framework that was performed at Drury Lane on April 15, 1740, probably through the good offices of Garrick's friend, Charles Macklin, who played the Drunken Man. It was enthusiastically received and became a staple of the repertory throughout Garrick's career. In March, 1742, after his initial appearance at Goodman's Fields, Garrick appeared in the title role of *The Lying Valet,* a clever farce of his own composition, which also remained a popular part of the repertory.

Playwriting was completely natural to Garrick, a basic and even necessary extension of his sensitive theatrical instincts. George Winchester Stone, Jr., has noted that Garrick's cardinal guiding principle in playwriting "(and doubtless the basis for the success of his plays and adaptations) derives from the inextricable combination in him of playwright *and* actor."[5] The actor's intelligence was never far from the playwright's technique as Garrick penned his works. In playwriting, his conception of character was molded by the actor's experiential knowledge of what the audience would accept as credible; his scenes of emotion were geared to the modulations of the human voice;

his creation of dialogue was paced to the realities of audience reaction; and his requirements for stage business were modified by the actor's instinct for effective physical movement.

Garrick wrote and adapted plays throughout his lengthy career. In all, he authored twenty-one original works; he collaborated with George Colman on one, *The Clandestine Marriage;* and he adapted twenty-six others. His last play, *May Day; or, The Little Gypsy,* was performed on October 28, 1775, less than eight months before his retirement.

**The Union of Talents: Playwright, Actor, Manager.** Garrick's natural talents as playwright were strengthened by his activities and experiences not only as actor, but also as manager. At the height of his career he was undeniably the most famous and most important theatrical personality of his age, known and applauded by his countrymen; acknowledged, sometimes grudgingly, by his antagonists; and exalted by continental Europeans. Garrick became so clearly identified with favorite roles, such as Abel Drugger and Hamlet, that scarcely another actor attempted them during the span of Garrick's career. In Edmund Burke's famous phrase: "He raised the character of his profession to the rank of a liberal art."[6]

As manager of the Theatre Royal at Drury Lane, Garrick's activities were more complex than artistic. He attained uncommon success in that position largely due to his sound business instincts and his enduring capacity for hard work. He purchased a half-interest in the theater for £8000 from John Lacy, and the two became equal partners. Their contract assigned Garrick responsibility for "setting or altering the business of the Stage," whereas Lacy had charge of "the economy of the household."[7] Although they were not close friends, the two observed the terms of the agreement with considerable respect and they continued together until Lacy's death in 1774. Garrick's brother, George, six years his junior, assisted him in the management of the theater, dealing with actors, authors, and house servants and serving as a valued confidante.[8]

Although Garrick's overall record of accomplishment as manager of Drury Lane is awesome, he was beset by difficulties throughout his tenure. Perhaps the most wearing of these was the attack of a group of young men who called themselves "The Town," who, over a period of approximately two years, opposed the manager's efforts to abolish the custom of admitting patrons after the third act of the mainpiece for half-price. Organized by Thaddeus Fitzpatrick, a long-time opponent of Garrick, they rioted on January 25, 1763, breaking the chandeliers in the theater and causing the cancellation of the evening's scheduled play. Garrick was forced to capitulate and retain the half-price custom.

This public humiliation seemed to crystallize Garrick's emotional and physical exaustion after almost sixteen years of cajoling performers, pleasing audiences, and soothing rejected playwrights. He decided upon an extended vacation from the theater and, with Mrs. Garrick, traveled to the Continent in September, 1763, for a lengthy holiday. There he enjoyed the adulation of continental Europeans and he returned to London in April, 1765, healthy, refreshed, and cunning, having arranged to publish, on the day of his arrival, "The Sick Monkey," an autobiographical fable in verse which served notice upon his opponents that he would deal expeditiously with their criticism.

Garrick thus resumed his theatrical life with renewed energy, completing work on *The Clandestine Marriage,* which he had begun with George Colman, and writing both original works and adaptations. In 1769, when his popularity and success had again peaked, he planned a spectacular, multifaceted celebration in honor of Shakespeare, which was to include both theatrical and extratheatrical elements.

The Shakespeare Jubilee was announced publicly by Garrick in May, 1769, to be held at Shakespeare's birthplace, Stratford-on-Avon, on September 6–8, 1769. As Garrick envisioned it, the jubilee was to be an exciting three-day tribute to England's greatest playwright, at which Englishmen could gather at the Bard's birthplace to honor him through music and merrymaking, and through poetry, horseracing, and fireworks. Garrick wrote a lengthy and dignified "Ode upon Dedicating a Building and Erecting a Statue to Shakespeare" and engaged Dr. Thomas Augustus Arne to set it to music. He asked Charles Dibdin to compose a score for a series of simple poems he had written in ballad style, and he planned the building of a Rotunda in the meadow on the banks of the Avon. Garrick even threw the energies of his Drury Lane staff into adapting the interior of the Rotunda for theatrical performances.

Thousands of Englishmen, men and women of all classes, the great and the ordinary, responding to the extensive publicity that the Shakespeare Jubilee had been given through the summer months, descended upon the ill-prepared small town of Stratford on September 5 for the celebrations which were scheduled for the sixth, seventh, and eighth. Unfortunately, overcrowding at the inns, overcharging

by local merchants, and an overabundant rainfall on the second day
of the festival dimmed the general mood of merrymaking and forced
the cancellation of several events which had taken months of prepa-
ration, among them the grand procession of the chief Shakespearean
characters. Garrick's elaborate scheme had failed, leaving him with a
debt of £2000.[9] But with characteristic business acumen and good
humor, he wrote the events of the Jubilee into a humorous musical
afterpiece entitled *The Jubilee* (1769), bringing it within six weeks to
Drury Lane where it became one of his notable successes.

His energies continued at a high level throughout the second half
of his career, and he attained new heights of success in presenting a
radically altered *Hamlet* in 1772 and a lively original farce, *Bon Ton,*
in 1775. Although he accepted only one new acting role after his return from the Continent in 1765, he continued to mesmerize his audiences with the performances of characters for which he had become
celebrated, such as Abel Drugger in Jonson's *The Alchemist,* Benedick
in Shakespeare's *Much Ado About Nothing,* and Lusignan in *Zara,* his
own adaptation of Voltaire's *Zaire.* In the last two months of his theatrical career he was careful to play all of his most celebrated roles at
least once and retired on June 10, 1776, to the overwhelming applause and affection of his London audience.

Even after his retirement Garrick continued to oblige the requests
of friends and associates for prologues and epilogues and performed a
reading of his works for the Royal Family, at Windsor. Although he
attempted to keep a full schedule, visiting friends and lending encouragement and advice to young actors and actresses, he was plagued
by illness and the gradual deterioration of his health. He died at
home on January 20, 1779, less than three years after his retirement.
Mrs. Garrick made the following entry in her journal: "At a quarter
before eight, my Husband sighed, and Died without one uneasy moment, the Lord be Praised."[10]

**Garrick's Contribution to Theatrical Art.**    Garrick's contribution to theater extended even beyond the writing of crowd-pleasing
plays and beyond the dazzling performances on stage for which he
became world-renowned; he made immense contributions to the development of theatrical art. Because he possessed a comprehensive and
thoughtful view of the role of theater in a civilized society, his central
concern during the twenty-nine years of his leadership was to elevate
the public taste at the same time that he provided sufficient entertainment for the broad-based audience to enable Drury Lane to main-

tain financial stability. By restoring a number of authentic Shakespearean texts to the stage, by using technically sophisticated music, rather than the simple melodies previously used in popular theater, and by restoring and adapting serious plays of other dramatists, Garrick did much to satisfy the first part of his objective, to elevate the taste of his audience. To capture the broad-based audience without compromising his artistic integrity, he produced plays of all types, both as mainpieces and afterpieces. Comedies, tragedies, farces, entertainments, musicals, masques, and pantomimes were presented at a prodigious rate so that almost fifty percent more new plays were presented at Drury Lane than at the rival theater at Covent Garden during the same period.

Tirelessly searching for new and more effective modes of theatrical expression, Garrick became an innovator in stage practice. Following his continental trip he introduced into the English theater stage lighting that was not visible to the audience. Garrick rid the stage of the overhanging chandeliers, upgraded the footlights, and used side-wing lights, in the manner of the French theater. A writer for the *Public Advertiser* (September 25, 1765) enthusiastically noted the innovation, stating that "the Drury Lane Managers have absolutely created an Artificial day . . . they seem to have brought down the Milky Way to the bottom of the Stage."

In 1772 Garrick added to the staff of the Drury Lane Theatre Philippe Jacques de Loutherbourg, an Alsatian artist who successfully experimented with colored lights, improved the use of stage transparencies, and brought in a new spirit of freedom in stage design. De Loutherbourg has come to be acknowledged as the most important and influential designer of the eighteenth-century English theater.

Another factor in Garrick's managerial success was his quick perception of changes in audience taste, perhaps best demonstrated in his changing attitude toward musical plays. Although he himself was not devoted to music, he sensed that his audiences were becoming increasingly appreciative of it and he significantly increased its presence at Drury Lane during his tenure as manager. He wrote numerous musical plays himself and staged many of other authors.

During his years of delicate dealings with actors and actresses, Garrick maintained remarkably good relationships with most of them, forming especially close friendships with the comedian Tom King and with the clever comic actress Kitty Clive, whom he nicknamed

"Clivey-Pivey." He went to great pains to support new young talent, once writing a part in *The Enchanter* expressly to introduce a promising vocal talent, Michael Leoni, and, another time, writing *May Day* to introduce a seventeen-year-old singer, Harriet Abrams.

Garrick endeared himself to his theatrical colleagues through the generous support he gave them for benefit-night performances. The benefit was the designated night when a specified player, author, or house employee was allowed to keep the receipts from ticket sales for himself, after paying the manager a minimal sum for house services and special lighting, music, or costumes. If the subject of a benefit chose a play that was popular with his audience, he might make the equivalent of two month's salary in one evening. Realizing this, Garrick sometimes put his talent at the services of his players and introduced a new play on a benefit night to draw a larger house. Garrick's farce *The Male Coquette* was devised to lend glitter to Henry Woodward's benefit night in 1757. For the lovely Hannah Pritchard, he wrote the popular interlude *The Farmer's Return from London* in 1761, and, for the comedian Tom King, he composed another interlude, *Linco's Travels,* in 1762.

On the last night of his professional career Garrick delivered "An Occasional Prologue" soliciting alms for infirm actors and actresses and turned the entire proceeds of the house over to that cause.

An examination of Garrick's busy and productive life, within and without the theater, reveals the warmth and good-humored wit that are reflected in his plays. An inveterate letter-writer, Garrick corresponded with hundreds of friends and acquaintances, discussing matters of both great and minute interest. A lively social presence, he was welcomed at gatherings of the prestigious and privileged who prized his sparkling conversation. "It is a dish of all sorts," said Samuel Johnson, "but of all good things."[11] An eighteenth-century gentleman, Garrick could pen a verse compliment to a lady with the same grace and ease with which he wrote a battery of theatrical prologues and epilogues. His life amply reflects those elements that distinguish his plays: ready wit, verbal cleverness, consistency of viewpoint, and high moral tone.

## Chapter Two

# The Playwright as Social Commentator: The Farces and Satires

In the course of his bold and innovative theatrical career David Garrick was an astute and amused observer of London. He scrutinized both the men and women of quality, who appeared to dominate the milieu, and the sensible but somehow awkward country gentry, who seemed to find it incomprehensible. He watched the dandies and the braggarts and cowards who peopled the important social gatherings, as well as the poor farmers who journeyed to the great city for a once-in-a-lifetime visit. He noted the coquettes and ingenues as well as the high-spirited, fun-loving young men about town.

Eleven light comedies, written over thirty-five years resulted from his observations. All of them were intended to serve as afterpieces, short plays designed to complete the evening's entertainment and to send the audience home in a pleasant mood. The use of afterpieces, introduced as an occasional practice early in the century, had gained increasing popularity as the century progressed, and, during Garrick's years as manager of Drury Lane from 1747 to 1776, the afterpiece was an expected part of the evening's entertainment. At London's two patent theaters patrons were accustomed to an evening's program that included a full-length mainpiece, diverting entr'acte entertainment, such as favorite songs, novelty dances, or instrumental performances, as well as the light and humorous two-act afterpiece. So popular were the afterpieces that spectators were admitted to the theater after the third act of the mainpiece for half-price to watch the conclusion of the principal play, the entertainment of the entr'acte, and the afterpiece. Because afterpieces were directed to a broader-based audience than the mainpieces, which were the staples of the evening's entertainment, they can be considered "a touchstone of eighteenth-century popular taste."[1]

Garrick's unfailing instinct for discerning what his audience wanted contributed to several substantial successes among his eleven original plays. *Lethe,* written and produced when Garrick was a struggling, unknown twenty-three-year-old actor unable to obtain an acting job in London's patent theaters, remained on the boards well into the nineteenth century and was one of his favorite pieces, both as playwright and actor. *The Lying Valet,* a lively farce written only two years later, also enjoyed distinguished success, receiving over four hundred performances during the century. *Miss in Her Teens,* a high-spirited comedy on the amours of a clever and practical young lady, delighted audiences for decades. *Bon Ton,* a genial satire on the false standards of behavior that dominated the social life of the town, was a product of Garrick's later career; its popular success demonstrated his ability to persuade the London theater audience to laugh at itself and its own foibles, without taking offense.

All of Garrick's plays are vitalized by his distinctive dramatic traits: fast-paced dramatic action, effective timing, careful craftsmanship, the use of topical material specifically directed to an English playhouse audience, and urbanity and wit in upholding the values of a civilized society.

Many of his plays are derivative, borrowing adroitly from the tradition of French farce, from predecessors on the English stage, and from a classic of English nondramatic literature, *Gulliver's Travels.* Like many eighteenth-century writers, Garrick respected the art of adaptation and imitation, which took material from masterpieces of the past to fashion it for acceptance by one's contemporaries. Writing to Mrs. Elizabeth Griffith on August 23, 1766, he explained his views: ". . . there can be no Objection to the introducing Circumstances, Incidents, Characters & Even Scenes that may bear some resemblance to old Plays, Authors should only take care that Such incidents Characters & Scenes are not too nearly Imitated, or ill-chosen."[2] Garrick not only chose well, but, perhaps more important, he stamped his individual imprint on his borrowings.

Garrick's eleven plays fall naturally into three groups: (1) those written from 1740 to 1747, during what may be described as a brilliant apprenticeship; (2) those written from 1757 to 1762, following his ten-year absence from playwriting; and (3) those written from 1766 to 1775, following his return from the Continent until his last season in the theater. One play, *The Clandestine Marriage* (1766), occupies a unique position in the Garrick canon because it was coauthored by Garrick and George Colman. Because scholarly evidence suggests that the play was both planned and written primarily by Garrick,[3] and because it reflects the same world depicted in the eleven individually written original comedies, *The Clandestine Marriage* will be included in this consideration of Garrick's original works. In their totality, Garrick's works show the progressive development of the facile young playwright into a seasoned dramatist with a sensitivity to social concerns and a flair for original conception.

## 1740–1747: The Brilliant Apprenticeship

During the first seven years of his theatrical career Garrick wrote *Lethe* (1740), *The Lying Valet* (1742), and *Miss in Her Teens* (1747), all works of enduring popularity. At this time he was enjoying the early successes of his acting career but was not yet encumbered with the responsibilities of managing Drury Lane. Given the freedom to concentrate on the art of playwriting, he diligently studied the theatrical repertory and derived substantial direction from the French theater.

*Lethe* (1740). Garrick's first play, *Lethe; or, Esop in the Shades,* both entertained and provoked its audience as the playwright focused a clear unfailing satiric gaze on eighteenth-century society. Lacking conventional dramatic structure, the one-act play is a series of conversations between Aesop, the renowned fabulist, and people of contemporary London. Aesop, generally revered by the classics-conscious eighteenth-century society as a repository of wisdom, stands at the center of the play and is immediately perceived as the dispenser of the reasonable point of view. Garrick is thus enabled to arrange a series of humorous and dramatically effective confrontations between the ancient voice of uncomplicated reason and contemporary society that basked in un-reason and self-indulgence.

Set in Hades on the anniversary of the rape of Proserpine, *Lethe* focuses on Aesop, who is called upon by Pluto to give freely the oblivion-granting waters of Lethe to careworn mortals. In the group of contemporary characters who are ferried across the Styx by Charon, London audiences recognized a failed playwright, a fine gentleman, a pair of unhappy newlyweds, a French marquis, and a lady of society.

Three of the most provocative characters, the Fine Gentleman, the French Marquis, and Mrs. Riot, serve to display the foibles of the town. The Fine Gentleman is a well-honed example of the false taste of the town, as he boasts to Aesop, ". . . I have skim'd the Cream of every Nation, and have the Consolation to declare, I never was in any Country in my Life, but I had Taste enough thoroughly to despise my own" (1.300–303).[4]

The French Marquis, actually a barber posing as a nobleman in order to marry an heiress, explains to Aesop why he is so well received by Londoners: "En fin, Sir, my Merit consists in one Vard—I am Foreignere" (1.467). He tells Aesop candidly that he would rather marry into a life of ease than return to France to eat soup and salad the rest of his life. Aesop's reply condemns London society, rather than the calculating barber: "I cannot blame you for your Choice; and if other People are so blind not to distinguish the Barber from the fine Gentleman, their Folly must be their Punishment" (1.515–17).

Mrs. Riot, loud, vulgar, and high-spirited, is the most fully developed character among Aesop's visitors. Her utter disregard of the fabulist's renown is evidenced in her greeting him as "you ugly Creature, you," and her vulgar provincialism is seen in her disappointment at the lack of social life in Hades. "What! no Operas! . . . Your Taste here, I suppose, rises no higher than your Shakespears and your Johnsons" (1.549–52). A precursor of Sheridan's Mrs. Malaprop, Mrs. Riot sees herself as "the very Quincettence and Emptity of a fine Lady," and her description of the pleasures of her life spills into a song, "The Midnight hark-away."

After a number of encounters with other members of London society, including a ninety-year-old man, a drunken man, and a tailor, Aesop is forced to conclude that his stories have had very little effect on the human race. He convenes the entire group, and, giving them advice characteristic of Garrick's moral tenor, he urges them to drink to the forgetfulness of vice, for " 'Tis Vice alone, disturbs the human Breast;/ Care dies with Guilt; be virtuous, and be blest" (1.824–25).

Although it is virtually plotless, *Lethe* was a successful afterpiece for more than thirty-five years; it maintained its popularity both because it was a splendid acting vehicle that was usually favored with distinguished and popular performers and because Garrick, as playwright, used the loose, episodic structure of the play to its best advantage by changing the dialogue and adding and deleting characters at various times to catch the public fancy. By 1741, two additional characters, a Frenchman and an Irishman, were added to the cast and the play became a favorite piece for benefit performances. After 1749, when Garrick was firmly entrenched as manager of Drury Lane, he himself began to play the roles of the failed playwright, the Frenchman, and the Drunken Man. Charles Adams enthusiastically described his characterizations in a letter to John Gilbert-Cooper as performed "most inimitably."[5] Observing the changes that had taken place in the dramatic text, Richard Cross, the prompter for Drury Lane, recorded in his Diary for January 2, 1749, "This farce of *Lethe* was wrote some years ago and play'd with Success, & was reviv'd this Night with great Alterations."[6]

Garrick continued to tailor his play to public taste, enlarging it in 1756 by adding the character of Lord Chalkstone, a man-about-town who provides a running commentary on contemporary London manners to Aesop, and a "New Mimic Italian song" sung by Mrs. Riot. The role of Lord Chalkstone became a favorite of Garrick's and remained so until the end of his career. Alluding to the interdependence of Garrick's playwriting and acting talents, Arthur Murphy astutely noted: "Which had most merit, the actor or the writer, was a question that the best critics could not decide."[7]

The process of revising *Lethe* continued and in 1772 Garrick provided additional characters: Fribble, a Methodist tailor, and a newly written Irishman to replace the Irishman who had been dropped in an earlier revision, and he altered the roles of Mr. and Mrs. Tatoo, renaming them Mr. and Mrs. Carbine. The fact that Garrick's play was not original in its broad outline lent no discredit to it as a popular success. It was indebted in part to John Vanbrugh's *Aesop* (1697) and to James Miller's unsuccessful *An Hospital for Fools* (1739); the latter was indebted to Vade's *l'Hôpital des Foux*. Garrick's play has, in addition, some tenuous ties to Molière's *Les Précieuses ridicules*. Garrick's talent lay in the flexibility with which he could utilize the outlines of existing material as the basis for his own dramatic sketch of contemporary London. The authenticity of his characterizations of well-known London types distinguished the play, and his use of song to heighten mood, such as Mrs. Riot's song on the life of a fine lady and her later Italian mimic piece, met with favorable audience reaction. Finally, the presentation of a universal moral, urbanely presented by Aesop, " 'Tis Vice alone, disturbs the human Breast . . .," addressed the audience directly and served to foreshadow the moral tone of later Garrick plays.

**The Lying Valet** (1742). Garrick's second play, *The Lying Valet,* was an immediate and striking success, delighting the audiences at Goodman's Fields with its fast-moving plot and lively dialogue. Popular for the remainder of the century, it was performed an astonishing 369 times during Garrick's career, the playbill often indicating that the play was presented either "By Command" of the King and Queen or "By desire" of several influential members of London society.

The plot turns upon the indigence of the likable, basically goodhearted Gayless, who has allowed himself to be misled by false friends and has, thereby, squandered his fortune. He plans to marry the beautiful and wealthy Melissa, whom he genuinely loves, on the following day, but feels conscience-bound to tell her of his true financial condition. His clever valet, Sharp, urges him to hold his tongue until after the wedding.

But the situation is complicated by Melissa's request that Gayless host a ball and entertainment on the eve of their wedding. The message is delivered by Kitty, Melissa's pert maid, who is a formidable match for Sharp in wit and cunning. The play unfolds as a series of hilarious scenes as Sharp attempts to cancel the feast, which his master cannot pay for. His impudence is seen in his attempt to convince Melissa that there has been talk of immoral behavior between her and Gayless. In addition, he suggests that she will compromise her reputation further by another visit to the home of Gayless. He tells her further that he has falsely confessed: "That my master loves fornication; that you had no aversion to it; that Mrs. Kitty was a bawd, and your humble servant a pimp" (1.2. 106–7). Although Melissa agrees not to attend the banquet, she requests that it be held as scheduled and plans to attend disguised as Mrs. Gadabout's nephew.

Comedy is high as the impeccably gracious Gayless and his resilient servant Sharp, with neither furniture nor provisions, strain to entertain Mrs. Gadabout, her daughter and her niece, Mr. Justice Guttle, and Mr. and Mrs. Trippit. These are humors characters in the traditional sense: each has a characteristic eccentricity which Garrick expresses through the individual's name. Mrs. Gadabout adds to the calamity by announcing that her nephew, newly returned from France, will soon join them.

The actions of Sharp, as he desperately tries to prepare a meal from an empty cupboard, provide high-spirited, bustling farcical action. He attempts to flatter Mrs. Gadabout's supposed nephew, not recognizing that he is Melissa in male disguise, by telling her ". . . there is something in your face that is generous, open, and masculine" (2.1.285–86). That failing, he indulges in gossip, describing his master's fiancée as ". . . none of the mildest or wisest of her sex" (2.1.308).

Sharp's connivings, bizarre, hilarious, but unsuccessful, are interrupted by the arrival of a drunken cook who apears with a wholly prepared meal, apparently confused as to his whereabouts. When the cook demands immediate payment for the meal, even the financially embarrassed Gayless is forced to ask money of the supposed nephew, who, pretending to have "a very great regard" for Melissa, challenges him to a duel. Gayless draws on him, but Kitty brings the action to a halt by blurting out that the young man is actually Melissa.

The final scene is one of soothing reconciliation. Melissa forgives Gayless, explaining that her intent was simply "to tease you a little that you might have a greater relish for a happy turn in your affairs" (2.1.492–94). She also reveals that a letter she had received earlier from her fiancé's father carried the forgiveness of the elder Gayless. All ends happily as Melissa calls for a dance and Gayless begins to savor this "most pleasing calm of perfect happiness."

The reasons for the success of the farce are not difficult to discern. The fast-paced action and sharp dialogue emanate naturally from the principal characters. Sharp and Kitty, clever, resourceful servants imported from the French farce tradition, are likable and lively. Gayless, basically good-hearted, is close to a sentimental hero who admits the error of his ways at the very beginning of the play. His difficulties have been brought on by an overreliance on the advice of others, rather than any malicious actions. His goal is a stable marriage to Melissa and the recapturing of a life of virtue. Throughout the play he is the exponent of good taste, graciousness to others, and the moral point of view. Melissa, however, is a more original creation. She is beautiful, wealthy, and genuinely in love; in her vitality, she seems to anticipate Kate in Goldsmith's *She Stoops to Conquer*. The clever use of humors characters as guests at Gayless's party heightens the comedy as they, in their complete predictability and woodenness, lend themselves perfectly to the wildly improbable party situation.

As a practical and practicing dramatist, Garrick saw the opportunities in this play for bringing together effective dramatic writing and fine theatrical performance. He himself played the role of Sharp to comic perfection in the first performance and kept it in his repertory for many years. Writing to his brother Peter in December, 1741, the playwright was exuberant about both text and performance: ". . . the valet takes prodigiously, & is approv'd of by Men of genius & thought yᵉ Most diverting Farce that ever was perform'd; I believe You'll find it read pretty well, & in performance 'tis a general Roar from beginning to End."[8]

Like Garrick's first play, *Lethe, The Lying Valet* was strongly derivative. It bears a close resemblance to the plot of Peter Motteux's *All Without Money,* a one-act playlet which formed the second act of his diverting program, *Novelty* (1697). *All Without Money,* performed only once, is described in its preface as "an Imitation of a part of a diverting French Comedy of one Act (for such plays are very common in Foreign Parts)."[9] The "diverting French comedy" which Motteux refers to is *Le Souper mal-apprêté* by Noël de Breton, sieur de Hauteroche, which was popular on the Parisian stage. The principal differences among the three plays are those of emphasis. The Hauteroche hero is utterly cynical, whereas Motteux's hero promises to reform at the end of the play. Garrick's Gayless, appropriate to his times, is sentimentally depicted, announcing his reform at the beginning of the play and serving as spokesman for the moral point of view throughout. Even the cunning Sharp, in Garrick's epilogue, appeals to sentimental values, excusing his own falsehoods: "For, though my tongue was false, my heart was true," while he attacks lying in medicine, law, and private life. In addition, Garrick added his own hallmarks of good timing, fast-paced dialogue, and a humorous attack upon the foibles of the town to his borrowed plot.

Less explicitly, Garrick was influenced by Ben Jonson and the humors tradition in theatrical comedy. He recognized the effectiveness and enduring popularity of Jonson and was sympathetic to Jonson's dramatic purposes, believing, with the earlier writer, that the entertainment value of comedy should not preclude its serving as a corrective mirror to society.[10] Underlying the effective comic scenes of *The Lying Valet* was an attack on extravagance, foppery, and prodigality. Central to Garrick's play is the articulation of a moral and reasonable point of view by the good-hearted Gayless.

One may conclude from an analysis of Garrick's indebtedness to earlier dramatists that he saw plot as the mere skeleton of the play. Both eclectic and practical in his approach to theater, he familiarized himself with successful theater, both in London and Paris, and felt himself entitled to draw freely upon whatever plot, characterizations, or gambits had succeeded earlier in order to refashion them to the needs and desires of his contemporary audience. His genius was synthetic rather than original and his theatrical acumen was largely unsurpassed in his day.

**Miss in Her Teens** (1747). *Miss in Her Teens,* a bright little farce first presented at Covent Garden on January 17, 1747, was Garrick's third consecutive success and was further demonstration of his theatrical talent. His instinct for identifying a play that would provide a congenial wedding of dramatic and theatrical excellences was again evident. *Miss in Her Teens* shows Garrick as a developing young playwright, able to capitalize upon the techniques that had brought him success in earlier works, yet becoming more masterful in his sense of plot structure and more original in his conception of character.

The play consists of only three scenes, all lean in construction and economical in expression. Captain Loveit, young, handsome, and resourceful, has had a brief acquaintance with Biddy Bellair prior to his military service and, during the long period of their separation, has come to love her. Unfortunately, he had been introduced to her and her family only as Rhodophil and, when he returns to her country home to resume their friendship, he learns that she has moved to town. His wily servant, Puff, whose wife, Tag, also lives in town, is engaged to learn the whereabouts of Biddy; the first act is the story of his success. In the course of his investigations Puff learns that Biddy, who is under the guardianship of her aunt, is engaged to marry an old gentleman. Despite this, the meeting of Biddy and Rhodophil is arranged by Puff by the end of the act. The only drawback is that two other beaux, whom Biddy has encouraged in order to prevent boredom, have been invited to visit her at the same time.

Tag, the cunning servant who knows Biddy's mind, has persuaded her aunt that the young girl should not be forced into a marriage; the aunt has agreed that Biddy may marry whom she pleases and may dispose of her old gentleman at his next visit. In a masterpiece of theatrical timing the much-mentioned beaux, Fribble and Captain Flash, enter separately early in the second act. Fribble, an effeminate, overly fastidious young suitor, arrives first, presenting Biddy with some of his very own lip-salve. In a self-revealing passage Fribble describes his circle of effeminate young men: "There is a club of us, all young bachelors, the sweetest society in the world, and we meet three times a week at each other's lodgings, where we drink tea, hear the chat of the day, invent fashions for the ladies, make models of 'em and cut out patterns in paper. We were the first inventors of knotting, and this fringe is the original produce and joint labor of our little community" (2.1.116–22).

Fribble's courtship of Biddy, which includes his singing a poem to her, is interrupted unceremoniously by the arrival of the braggart Captain Flash, and Fribble is scurried off to be hidden in the storeroom. The soldier's opening lines identify him as the perfect foil for Fribble's fastidiousness: he is bombastic, bold, and swaggering. Immediately, he wants to set the wedding date for Biddy and himself, answering Biddy's tame objections to his status: "I study the Book of Fate, and the Camp is my University" (2.1.251–52).

Biddy cleverly directs the action to a point where Flash realizes he has a rival and is virtually forced to duel Fribble. In one of the finest comic scenes Garrick has written both unwilling swains assume fighting postures but are virtually frozen into position by their cowardice. Biddy and Tag hover around them, attempting to push them forward. The superb physical comedy is interrupted by the arrival of Captain Loveit and Puff, who rid Biddy of her would-be swains. Recognizing Flash as a military deserter, Loveit gives him a swift kick and forbids him to wear the uniform in the future but merely dismisses Fribble, who is "too despicable for Correction."

There is yet another disguise scene as Captain Loveit and Puff are forced to hide, upon the arrival of the elder suitor. Biddy, whose pleasure has been heightened by the events of the afternoon and who realizes she is acting within the purview of her aunt's permission, becomes very flippant with the old gentleman. Telling him of Captain Loveit, she slaps him on the back and suggests that he challenge the Captain, who is now the reigning victor. In the final scene Captain Loveit enters and recognizes the suitor as his father. The elder Loveit gracefully withdraws his suit, and the romance of the soldier and the high-spirited coquette is free to proceed. Biddy steps forward to give a cautious directive to the ladies of the town: "Ladies, to Fops and Braggarts ne'er be kind" (2.1.602).

In an incisive commentary on the play Arthur Murphy, a contemporary of Garrick, explained why the audience found the characterizations of Fribble and Captain Flash authentic. "*Captain Flash* and *Fribble* are not the mere offspring of the poet's imagination, they were copied from life. The coffee-houses were infested by a set of young officers, who entered with a martial air, fierce *Kavenhuller* hats, and long swords. They paraded the room with ferocity, ready to draw without provocation. In direct contrast to this race of braggarts, stood the pretty gentlemen, who chose to unsex themselves, and make a display of delicacy that exceeded female softness." Murphy continues, explaining Garrick's purpose: "To expose these two opposite characters to contempt and ridicule was the design of *Miss in Her Teens,* and this was effectually done by *Woodward,* in *Captain Flash,* and *Garrick* in the mincing character of *Fribble.* The ferocious, swaggering *Bravo* did not chuse to be called *Captain Flash,* and the delicate beau was frightened out of his little wits by the name of *Fribble.*" Murphy concludes definitively: "They were both laughed out of society."[11]

In his "Advertisement" to the play Garrick acknowledged his indebtedness to the French playwright, Florent Carton, sieur Dancourt, on whose play, *La Parisienne* (1691), Garrick had modeled his own. He invites comparison of the two plays by his readers to determine "whether the Plot and Characters are alter'd for the better or worse." Garrick lifts from Dancourt the seminal dramatic situation in which a young, high-spirited girl whose lover has long been absent encourages the attention of two unsuitable suitors merely to escape boredom and even allows herself to become engaged to marry an old gentleman. Garrick rearranges many of the circumstances of the French play in order to construct a first act that is masterful in its exposition. Beginning with Captain Loveit's admission of his passion for Biddy to his servant, to Puff's meeting his wife Tag, the action builds logically to the point where Tag is able to announce to Biddy an appointment that afternoon with Rhodophil, but is surprised to learn that Flash and Fribble will also be there.

The second act is also deftly constructed, built upon the four separate appearances of the four beaux. Concealments lead to broadly dramatic confrontations of the rivals, for example, Fribble and Flash in their comic dueling scene, and the Captain's shocked recognition of his father. Physical comedy is used effectively to link the various entrances and exits with plausibility, such as Captain Loveit's kicking of Flash, who thereupon runs offstage, and Biddy's later slapping the elder Loveit on the back in a mood of great flippancy, which leads to the entrance of the Captain.

In addition to using the Dancourt material as the basis for a well-structured playlet, Garrick also used it as the basis for his two great characterizations, Fribble and Captain Flash. Dancourt's play contains two beaux whom Garrick has transformed into contemporary London types, as Murphy has noted.

It is also possible, as the nineteenth-century theater historian John Genest points out, that Garrick extrapolated elements of comic situations from Thomas Baker's *Tunbridge Walks* (1729), a moderately successful play which had been performed the preceding season at Goodman's Fields. [12] *Tunbridge Walks* includes a duel scene and features two characters, Maiden and Captain Squib, who appear to be pallid forerunners of Fribble and Captain Flash.

As always, the essential consideration in evaluating Garrick's ability is the extent to which he focused on and individualized extant material to sculpt a play that pleased his audiences while satisfying his theatrical and ethical aims. He enhanced the text by casting his most talented performers in the play, taking the part of Fribble himself. *Miss in Her Teens* was an overwhelming success and became one of the most frequently presented afterpieces of the period. Its popularity extended to America where, as in London, it was performed throughout the entire century, demonstrating, as had *Lethe* and *The Lying Valet,* Garrick's talent for writing a play that is hilarious and eminently actable.

## 1757–1762: The Return to Playwriting

After ten years of failing to produce an original work, Garrick returned to playwriting with *Lilliput* (1757), and followed this with *The Male Coquette* (1757), *The Guardian* (1759), and *The Farmer's Return from London* (1762). After accepting the managership of Drury Lane in 1747, Garrick had devoted himself for the next decade to the responsibilities of that position and to the task of adapting works, both Shakespearean and non-Shakespearean plays, for the stage. The experience had provided invaluable education in playcrafting, and Garrick returned to the writing of original work with a sharpened awareness of dramatic technique and a broadened concern for social issues. In addition to using the French tradition Garrick, during this period, derived inspiration from English writers and wrote his first wholly original piece, *The Farmer's Return from London.*

**Lilliput** (1757).    In writing *Lilliput* Garrick looked beyond the theater to an English satire that had, within thirty short years of its publication, become recognized as a masterpiece. Garrick's choice was sound for Jonathan Swift's *Gulliver's Travels* was not only esteemed by serious-minded thinkers for its probing of essential problems but had, by mid-century, become known in considerable detail even by those who were not well educated, and incidents and characters from the *Travels* were part of the cultural currency of the time.

Garrick might well have modified Swift's well-known attitude to state that his aim was both to divert and to vex his audience. Exploiting the popularity of *Gulliver's Travels,* Garrick's *Lilliput* had the force of an eighteenth-century morality play. Wisely, the dramatist chose "The Voyage to Lilliput," the most fanciful, most delicate, and best-known part of *Gulliver's Travels* to adapt to stage presentation. Specifically, Garrick selected incidents from chapters 5, 6, and 7 of Book I as the material for his one-act play, which satirizes marital behavior in London. Garrick's prologue sharply focuses the attack in true Swiftian fashion by issuing a disclaimer: "To you these little folks have no relation,/ As different in their manners as their nation,/ To show your pranks requires no conjuration" (32–34).

In Garrick's *Lilliput* Flimnap is a detached, urbane modern husband who has summoned his wife's two brothers, Bolgolam and Fripperel, in order to discuss his wife's indiscretion in falling in love with Gulliver. Shocked, Bolgolam comments on the influence on Lilliputian manners of the neighboring kingdom of Blefescu: "Time was when we had as little vice here in Lilliput as any where; but since we imported politeness and fashions from Blefescu, we have thought of nothing but being fine gentlemen: and a fine gentleman, in my dictionary, stands for nothing but impertinence and affectation, without any one virtue, sincerity, or real civility" (1.29–34).

The brothers' reaction to the news of their sister's misbehavior demonstrates the contrast between them. Bolgolam, Lord High Admiral of the Lilliputian Navy, is a spokesman for the good old English ways and is incredulous, whereas Fripperel, a dandified young Englishman in the tradition of Fribble, is intrigued by the idea. He asks Flimnap for evidence: ". . . have you caught her in his sleeve, or coat pocket? or has she been lock'd up in his snuff-box?" (1.88–89). But Bolgolam disregards this apparent flippancy and counsels a direct confrontation between Gulliver, as lover, and Flimnap, as husband. Gulliver, he decides, must be driven out of the kingdom in order to protect his sister's reputation. He is unaware of the fact that Lord Flimnap is not entirely unhappy over his wife's straying affections, for he believes, as the aggrieved husband, he will be implicitly released from the obligation of marital fidelity. The action becomes more complicated when Fripperel intercepts a love letter from Moretta to the scheming husband, Flimnap, and decides to copy its contents first and then present the letter to him publicly.

Finally the audience becomes acquainted with Gulliver, who appears disconsolate, although he has been recently elevated to the position of Nardac. Having become disenchanted with the delicacy and ingenuity of the Lilliputians, he now perceives that they are not essentially different from eighteenth-century Englishmen. He muses: "Every thing is in miniature here but vice; and that is so disproportioned, that I'll match our little rakes at Lilliput with any of our finest gentlemen in England" (3.35–37).

The pointedness of *Lilliput*'s message is softened by the physical comedy reminiscent of Henry Fielding's *Tom Thumb* in the scene between Gulliver and Lady Flimnap. Her description of the ladies of quality strikes the same target that had been hit by Mrs. Riot in *Lethe* and by Fribble in *Miss in Her Teens:* "It is below a woman of quality to have either affection or economy; the first is vulgar and the last is mechanic" (3.85–87). When her passionate declarations of love for Gulliver are met by his unimpassioned, logical arguments on the disproportion of their sizes, she answers with good-natured resiliency that love is a great leveler. But when he argues further that he loves his wife and six children who are waiting for him in England, her passion turns to rage and she instinctively sacrifices Gulliver's reputation when she is discovered in his apartment by her husband and brothers.

On the strength of her false accusations, the maligned Gulliver is scheduled to stand trial on the following day. Lady Flimnap gains further strength and general sympathy by exposing the contents of the love letter from Moretta, which is now publicly delivered to her husband. But when the news arrives that Gulliver, sensing his imminent destruction, has escaped to Blefescu with Bolgolam's ship, Flimnap and his wife are perforce reconciled and vow to begin their marriage anew, this time each ominously promising the other total personal freedom. Fripperel blesses this, their second and, inevitably, happier union, but Bolgolam disowns them all and vows to return to sea.

The drama has come full circle and nothing has changed. Indeed, the clear import of *Lilliput* is that nothing can change, for this is the way of the world. Nevertheless, laxity in personal morals, extravagances in the life of a lady of quality, and fulfillment of one's self at the expense of one's marital partner are made to seem ludicrous.

In an effort to combine authenticity and fantasy Garrick boldly recruited approximately one hundred young children whom he personally coached to play the role of the diminutive Lilliputians. Bransby, an actor in the Drury Lane company, played the part of Gulliver. Arthur Murphy commented on Garrick's innovation: "By introducing this fictitious race in a regular drama, Garrick saw that two important points might be attained. At the sight of such diminutive creatures, adopting the follies of real life, the fashionable world might learn to lower their pride, and the dignity of vice would be lost. At the same time, the public would enjoy their dear variety."[13]

Although Garrick's *Lilliput* did not match its three predecessors in sustained audience popularity, it was a successful theater piece and further demonstrated his versatility as a playwright. The play evidences his delight in theatrical experimentation as well as his practice of adapting material significant in the cultural milieu as the basis for stage presentation. *Lilliput* articulates, as did Garrick's three previous plays, a broadly stated moral directed to the theater audience in an attempt to elevate the mores of the town with wit and humor.

**The Male Coquette** (1757).   *The Male Coquette,* significantly subtitled *Seventeen Hundred Fifty-Seven,* is a gently satiric look at London high society in that year, accomplished through amusing characterizations and sharp dramatic encounters. Garrick's "Advertisement" announces that the play was written in haste to serve as a benefit performance for Henry Woodward and to oppose a group of young Londoners known as the Daffodils. It was a natural wedding of idea and personality: Henry Woodward, long a memorable harlequin, was Garrick's master comedian whose dominant stage presence had made him an appealing Mercutio and a swaggering Captain Flash; the Daffodils were the most recent grouping of young men of fashion whose self-indulgence and affectation had made them both ludicrous and offensive to Garrick.

After first titling the play *The Modern Fine Gentleman,* Garrick renamed it *The Male Coquette: or, Seventeen Hundred Fifty-Seven* in order to broaden its application and to suggest the scope and severity of the social blight caused by the Daffodils. He intended Daffodil to epitomize the unfeeling young man of fashion who is, nevertheless, attractive to women. Even the lovely Sophia Sprightly admits to having "a whimsical attachment" to him, so strong that it impels her to masquerade as a young Italian nobleman, believing that "the only way to find out his character is to see him thus and converse freely with him" (1.1.4–5).

As the Marchese di Macaroni, she visits Daffodil, finding him with Mrs. Dotterel, whom he is trying to discard. That lady has just upbraided him "for the poor reputation of having that which thou hast neither power nor spirit to enjoy" and leaves him to the allegedly male company that has just arrived. In conversation with the supposed Marchese, Daffodil explains his plan to discard the cousins, Sophia and Arabella, remarking coolly about Sophia: "Yes, poor creature; I believe she'll have a pang or two, tender indeed, and I believe will be unhappy for some time" (1.2.296–97). This is sufficient to persuade Sophia that Daffodil is "an abandoned, rash, profligate, male coquette, a wretch who can assume passions he never feels and sport with our sex's frailties" (2.1.8–10).

Later, at the Club-Room, where Daffodil receives an invitation to meet in secrecy an alleged female admirer who signs herself "Incognita," he happily assents, raising the rhetorical question, "Must a man be in love with every woman that invites him?" (2.2.143–44). In fact, Daffodil decides to make sport of Incognita's love for him by arranging with the other gentlemen: ". . . after I have been with her half an hour you'll come upon us and have a blow up." Incognita is, in fact, Sophia's faithful suitor, Tukely, disguised in female dress, who has positioned Daffodil's five current lovers behind trees on Birdcage Walk as he meets Daffodil, in order to reveal to them Daffodil's true nature.

In an effort to ingratiate himself with Incognita, Daffodil systematically attacks each of the five eavesdropping ladies: the Widow Damply is "past forty, wears a wig, and has lost two of her fore teeth . . . she looks for the world like a Great Mogul in petticoats." Mrs. Dotterel is "an idiot," while Lady Fanny Pewit "is an absolute old maid, Madam, almost as thick as she is long, middle-aged, homely and wanton." Even Sophia and her cousin, Arabella, are described as "poor silly, good-natured, loving fools. I made my addresses to one through pique and the other for pity" (2.3.60–112).

In the final scene Sophia, dressed in a surtout and slouched hat, pretending to be Incognita's enraged husband, joins Daffodil's gentlemen friends from the Club-Room and the five wronged ladies. All descend on Daffodil, sending him scurrying to the Opera and leaving

Tukely to articulate the moral to the ladies in the audience: to shun and detest "these destroyers of your reputation."

Much of the success of the play is due to Garrick's deft characterizations. Daffodil personifies the self-centeredness and foolishness of the young men of fashion. His description of his interest in women is revealing; he tells his valet, "A true sportsman has no pleasure but in the chase" (1.2.58), explaining to him that he has no intention of ruining the ladies to whom he has professed love. If, in fact, he ruins their reputations, "That's their business, not mine" (1.2.52). He reviews his list of female lovers enthusiastically, citing his most recent "acquisitions." He elaborates upon this philosophy in his first meeting with the supposed Marchese: "I am for variety and badinage without affection," for, he explains, "to ruin women would be troublesome; to trifle and make love to 'em amuses one" (1.2.254–57). Daffodil evidences the same lack of feeling toward his gentlemen associates as he does toward the ladies. In the Club-Room scene he cruelly mentions "pork" to his sickly cousin Dizzy, for the express purpose of making him nauseous. When Dizzy collapses, Daffodil calmly takes bets on whether his cousin will live until morning.

If his self-centeredness makes him unappealing, his folly makes him amusing. He is ready to share these follies with the Marchese, whom he believes a kindred spirit. He admits to him that he has lost substantially on horses; when he leads him into his study, he offers him the current entertainment of young gentlemen: in music, a guitar and Venetian ballads; in literature, "infidelity and bawdy novels." In a later scene at the Club-Room he foolishly bets large sums of money on preposterous antics: "The Honorable George Daffodil has betted one hundred pound with Sir William Whister that he produces a gentleman, before the 5th of June next, that shall live for five days successively without eating, drinking or sleeping" (2.2.40–44).

Sophia, in contrast to Daffodil, is intelligent, direct, spirited in her actions and active in the genteel investigation of a man to whom she is honestly attracted. She is determined to satisfy her own intelligence as to Daffodil's actions toward women and insists upon adopting the identity of Il Marchese di Macaroni, telling her cousin: "If I did not think a man's character was of some consequence, I should not now run such risks and encounter such difficulties to be better acquainted with it" (1.1.11–14). In her male guise she is an intentionally ludicrous figure. Daffodil's valet, Ruffles, describes his initial encounter with Macaroni thus: "He first capered out of the chair, and when I told him your honor was not at home, he capered into it again, said he would call again, jabbered something, and away he went singing" (1.2.117–20). But, at bottom, her expert mimicry has a very serious purpose and result. It acquaints her with Daffodil's value scheme and her former "whimsical attachment" soon turns to rage which, however, she tries to check: "I am vexed that I should be angry at him, when I should only despise him" (1.2.316–17). Sophia has the good sense to unite herself with her faithful suitor, Tukely, who, like her, is intelligent, candid, and civilized in his behavior. In fact, he mirrors Sophia's spirited actions by disguising himself as Incognita in the last scene.

The minor characters, only roughly sketched, are used to give definition to the lovers, Sophia and Tukely, and to the offensive and ludicrous Daffodil. The Club-Room scene, one of the finest theatrical moments in the play, introduces the audience to a host of characters no better than Daffodil. Together, the young men gamble, talk about women, drink champagne, and plot their amusements, creating an unsavory moral climate. Only Sir William behaves differently: he wants to send for the physician for the nauseous Dizzy and he refuses to participate in the plot to expose Daffodil's lady. Although his singular ways are dismissed lightly by the young men because "he's married and past fifty," his concern for others serves to underscore the self-centered antics of the young men of fashion. The ladies who have been individually courted and spurned by Daffodil serve as role models for the ladies of the audience whom Tukely cautions at the end of the play to beware the young men of fashion.

Garrick drew his inspiration for this play from a variety of sources within the English theatrical tradition. Daffodil may be traced in part to the braggart Captain Spark in Henry Fielding's *Universal Gallant* (1735), and in part to Horner in William Wycherley's *Country Wife* (1675). The ladies he has spurned are reminiscent of Lady Wishfort of William Congreve's *Way of the World* (1700) and Margery Pinchwife of *The Country Wife*.

*The Male Coquette* was an effective and diverting work that set its wholesome lovers against a background of Restoration schemes and values, embodied in Daffodil and his gentlemen friends. The dialogue throughout has something of the brilliance of repartee in Restoration comedy, but the moral center of the play lies wholly in the eighteenth century. The play became an audience favorite and was often used for benefit performances, Garrick himself using it for his benefit performance as author on December 12, 1757.

*The Guardian* (1759).   Garrick writes in the "Advertisement" to *The Guardian* that he is indebted to the *Pupille* of Monsieur Fagan, a playlet that had been called by Voltaire "the most complete Petite-Piece upon their stage.—It now appears in an English dress, with such alterations from the original as the difference of language and manners required." What clearly appealed to Garrick in Fagan's little work was the framework which enabled him to develop individual characters amid a grouping of amusing stock types and the situation which allowed him to comment on contemporary London mores.

Garrick uses the ingredients that he had combined deftly in his earlier successes: good-hearted central characters, adverse circumstances, and a happy ending. Harriet is the beautiful young heiress, direct, intelligent, and independent. Sir Charles Clackit expresses a consensus when he says, "This young lady has something very extraordinary about her" (2.1.336–37). In her quest for a serious love built upon genuine affection and compatibility of values, she is not unlike Sophia in *The Male Coquette;* in his sincerity and his steadfastness, Heartly, her beloved, is not unlike Tukely, Sophia's suitor. The cast of *The Guardian* is completed by Sir Charles Clackit, the kindly but blundering neighbor; Young Clackit, his ostentatious, dandified nephew; and Lucy, Harriet's coarse and clever servant. The love relationship between Harriet and Heartly, who is also her guardian, emerges at the end of the play. It had been submerged because of her natural modesty and maidenly reluctance and because of his wish not to take advantage of his legal situation as guardian. Thus far, Garrick has adapted Fagan's play accurately. However, it is in the characterization of the lovers that the playwright injects originality. Rather than the sympathetically drawn lovers of the French comedy, Garrick creates lovers who, in their exaggeration of the characteristics of the sentimental hero and heroine, burlesque the type.

The lack of candor about their mutual feelings has given the vain, self-satisfied Young Clackit the opportunity to press his suit for Harriet's hand. Though there have been no signs of affection from Harriet who, in fact, loathes him, he assures his well-meaning uncle, Sir Charles Clackit, that he has "proofs" of her love for him: "First, then—whenever I see her, she never looks at me. That's a sign of love. Whenever I speak to her, she never answers me—another sign of love. And whenever I speak to anybody else, she seems to be perfectly easy.—That's a certain sign of love" (1.1.34–37).

Sir Charles, though unpersuaded, agrees to bring his nephew's suit to the attention of his good friend and neighbor, Heartly. Both are mature men, Clackit, "a man of sixty-five, nay, just entering into his sixty-sixth year," and Heartly, "on the wrong side of forty," who are unsympathetic to Young Clackit's ludicrous ways but, believing that the young people may be in love, do what they can to formalize the situation. Harriet's confusion and embarrassment increase as she feels forced to confess her true feelings to Heartly in order to rid herself of the obnoxious Young Clackit. She decides to dictate a letter to Heartly, ostensibly for Young Clackit, but by its tone and content aimed at Heartly himself. She thus hopes to reveal her true feelings to Heartly, but he, failing to grasp its import, sends it to Young Clackit and Harriet finds herself too reticent to prevent it.

Lucy adds to the confusion by announcing that her mistress had admitted to her that "she settled her affections upon one of riper years and riper understanding" (2.1.191–92). She thus persuades Sir Charles Clackit that he is the object of Harriet's affections, a theory which, though preposterous, pleases the old gentleman. In the last scene, in which Harriet is on stage with the three men, she emphatically rejects Young Clackit and, more gently, his aged uncle. Heartly, now persuaded that it is he whom Harriet loves, admits the depth of his feelings for her and the play ends with the promise that "the fond husband still the Guardian prove."

The play moves quickly, exploiting its varied comic possibilities. The comedy of characterization is supplied in part by Young Clackit, vain, arrogant, prancing about stage with his looking glass, his lack of thought indicated by the songs he hums. He manages to disaffect all other characters, being dubbed "young Shatter-brains" by Lucy. It is his behavior that precipitates numerous attacks on the vanity and foolishness of the young men of London.

Lucy supplies the broad comedy in the scene in which she tells Sir Charles that, since Harriet had admitted loving an older man, it must be he. To persuade him of the depth of Harriet's feeling, she relates their morning's conversation: "Good God, Madam said I, why he is old and gouty, asthmatic, rheumatic, sciatic, spleenatic— It signified nothing; she had determined." To which Sir Charles quietly replies, "But you need not have told her all that" (2.1.208–11).

Lucy's final judgment on the impending match of Harriet and Heartly is voiced approvingly: "You have my taste exactly, Miss. Ripe fruit for my money: When it is too green it sets one's teeth on edge, and when too mellow it has no flavor at all" (2.1.362–64). Garrick developed Lucy's character so that she is more fully his creation than Fagan's.

The playwright's controlled use of dramatic irony informs what is perhaps the most effective scene in the play, that in which Harriet dictates the letter to Heartly. Harriet struggles to convey her true feelings to the man she loves, while still keeping within the restrictions of modesty assigned a young lady of the time:

> Harriet:   "Everything tells you that it is you that I love."
>
> Heartly:   Very well. (Writes)
>
> Harriet:   Yes—you "that I love," do you understand me?
>
> Heartly:   Oh, yes, yes, I understand you—"that it is *you* that I love." This is very plain my dear. (2.1.75–79).

The lovers function on two levels. Literally, they represent the respect for reason over passion, the concern for genteel good manners without the vulgarity of ostentation, and the regard for affection and compatible interests in marriage, all values which Garrick championed. More interestingly, perhaps, they are the *reductio ad absurdum* of the sentimental lovers, and they represent the keen-eyed dramatist's view of the disservice done good theater by playwrights who insisted on repeating and exaggerating the worn-out conventions of sentimental theater long after it could be seriously countenanced by an audience.

Garrick played Heartly and the play was received "with universal applause," according to Richard Cross, the Drury Lane prompter. After fourteen performances during its first season, *The Guardian* became a standard item in the afterpiece repertory and was played at least once every season until Garrick's retirement from the stage.

**The Farmer's Return from London** (1762).   Unlike *Lilliput, The Male Coquette,* and *The Guardian,* which were all afterpieces, *The Farmer's Return from London* was a short verse interlude, written as a favor to the popular actress, Hannah Pritchard, for her benefit night on March 20, 1762. The interlude was intended for a single night's performance, to be staged between two popular plays, Vanbrugh's *The Mistake* and Murphy's *The Old Maid.*

Written in dialect, the interlude depicts the return of the farmer from London, which he has visited to attend the "crownation" ceremonies of George III and Caroline, an event that had generated intense national interest and, therefore, made good topical fare for theater. The farmer's affectionate family anxiously absorb his interpretations of city life and willingly accept his description of London as "a fine hugeous city,/ Where the geese are all swans and the fools are all witty." They listen, too, to his description of the Cock Lane Ghost, another timely matter.[14]

*The Farmer's Return* was both sprightly and pointed in its remarks; thus, it won immediate popularity. Arthur Murphy noted that it was "hotly called for" after its first performance.[15] It was performed twelve times during the few weeks remaining in the 1761–62 season and revived during three additional seasons, altogether compiling a very creditable record for a brief, topical piece that had been intended for one night's performance only.

The success of *The Farmer's Return from London* lay in Garrick's expert manipulation of theatrical effects: the creation of low country types whose words speak more wisdom than they appear to realize; the vitality and fast pace of the descriptive verse; the lightness and good nature of the satirical thrusts; and the clever exploitation of events of intense topical interest.

## 1766–1775: The Mature Dramatist

Garrick returned from an eighteen-month tour of the Continent in 1765 personally refreshed and professionally educated through his exposure to the advanced technology of French theater. He brought the full weight of his powers to bear on playwriting and produced *Neck or Nothing* (1766), *The Irish Widow* (1772), *The Meeting of the Company* (1774), and *Bon Ton* (1775). Although he continued to derive inspiration from the French tradition, his last two works were wholly original.

**Neck or Nothing (1766).** Despite the fact that *Neck or Nothing,* Garrick's adaptation of Alain Le Sage's popular play, *Crispin,* was a more correct farce than some of his previous works, it failed to make a strong impact on the theatergoing public. Garrick, who did not place his name on the first edition, calls the piece "trifling" in his

"Advertisement" and dubs it "an imitation of the *Crispin Rival de Son Maître* of Le Sage."

As in his earlier adaptations and imitations, Garrick looked to the original work for situation and skeletal plot and then recast it to point the play toward the English public. The thoroughly improbable plot turns upon the fact that the wealthy citizen, Stockwell, has promised his lovely young daughter, Nancy, in marriage to Young Harlowe, son of Stockwell's good friend from the country, Sir Harry Harlowe. However, Young Harlowe must marry a young lady from Dorsetshire in order to save her reputation. Not only does this necessitate a change in the plans of the elders, but it allows the rascally servants, Martin and Slip, to engineer a fraud. When Slip, Harlowe's servant, arrives from the country to tell Stockwell of Young Harlowe's situation, he meets Belford's servant, Martin, and the two concoct a plan by which Martin will imitate Harlowe and the two will make off with the lady's fortune. But Nancy, who has never met Harlowe, is in love with Belford, a young gentleman about town, and is bent on using every means available to oppose the upcoming wedding.

Her resolution is firmed when Slip, disguised as Harlowe, engages in such awkward displays of excessive gallantry and attention to her mother that Nancy is convinced he is "an impertinent, absurd coxcomb." When Belford displays Harlowe's letter telling of his marriage, Slip cleverly convinces Stockwell that Belford has forged the letter because he himself wants to marry Nancy. The two rascals go on to convince Belford that Harlowe's marriage was called off and persuade Harlowe's father, Sir Harry, that Stockwell is enraged at the cancellation of the match. In the last scene, however, an enlightened Belford enters with the constables who seize Martin and Slip. The play ends quickly and happily, as Stockwell gives his blessing to Nancy's marriage to Belford and is reconciled to his old friend, Sir Harry.

Garrick's play has an abundant assemblage of ingredients for farce. Stereotypic characters effectively animate an unlikely plot suitable for absurd happenings. Physical comedy, a major ingredient of farce, is also abundant. Throughout, the characteristic Garrick hallmarks of fast-paced action and effective timing contribute to the effectiveness of the play.

Social commentary, though frequent in Garrick's plays, is noticeably missing from *Neck or Nothing*. Although there is an occasional remark about "the young fellows of this age" and a lone sally against the female sex, the play moves along briskly on its own momentum as a pure farce and does not look outwards to the London world.

Despite its technical strengths, *Neck or Nothing* was not one of Garrick's more popular works. He undoubtedly sensed that the unvarnished, bald, and somehow culturally remote antics of rogues and rascals had little interest for the English theatergoing public which, by the late eighteenth century, had many topical interests. In a letter to a fellow playwright, Herbert Lawrence, on January 10, 1774, Garrick writes of a minor change he had had to make in *Neck or Nothing* to make the character of Stockwell more plausible, explaining that "an audience will not Suffer the Dupe to be cheated too extravagantly even in a Farcical piece."[16]

Garrick ceased writing pure farce after *Neck or Nothing,* and concentrated on works that were concretely grounded in topics and themes of specific, contemporary interest to London audiences.

**The Irish Widow** (1772). *The Irish Widow,* Garrick's merry farce written specifically as an acting vehicle for Anne Barry, was an early and lasting success. He derived the basic outlines of his play from Molière's *Le Mariage forcé,* with perhaps some borrowings from his *L'Avare;* he added to the plot amusing characters who appealed to the overtly English tastes of his audience by directing the comedy against popular objects of satire: marriages of convenience and English chauvinistic patriotism.

The play focuses on Old Whittle, a man of sixty-five years, who has fallen in love with his nephew's fiancée, a lovely young Irish widow of twenty-three. Despite the advice of his good friend Bates, who urges him to return to his "woolen caps, flannel waistcoats, worsted stockings, cork soles, and galochys," Old Whittle determines to have the young widow, whom he had met on a trip to Scarborough. The trip was, ironically, arranged by the nephew so that his uncle, who is also his guardian, might meet the young lady of his choice, approve of her, and release his fortune. Old Whittle is the obvious butt of the comedy as he lies about his age, reads nothing but love poetry, and consoles himself that his friend Bates, who does not agree with him, is "old and peevish." The folly of his situation is paralleled by that of Old Kecksy, another elderly gentleman who insists that his recent marriage to a young woman has brought him happiness.

Against this background, the eminently sane Bates and the nephew unite to persuade the charming young widow that she must assume a new and offensive personality if she is to discourage Old Whittle from marrying her, the nephew arguing that ". . . if amidst all his rapturous ideas of your delicacy you would bounce upon him a wild, ranting, buxom widow, he will grow sick of his bargain and give me a fortune to take you off his hands" (1.2.42–45). The widow agrees and becomes, first, a coarse country wench who effectively embarrasses and discourages Old Whittle, and, later, imitates her brother, Lieutenant O'Neale, and angrily visits Old Whittle after he has written to the widow withdrawing from the planned marriage.

Young Whittle and the widow are not totally successful in their plot to secure Old Whittle's blessing on their marriage, the nephew's fortune, and an additional fortune of £5000 for the widow, because her father, Sir Patrick O'Neale, identifies her as his daughter masquerading as his son. Overcome by shame, Old Whittle blesses the union and relinquishes the nephew's fortune, but not the additional sum. The delighted widow philosophically declares: "Though we have not so much money, we shall have more love" (2.1.457–58) and the play ends merrily to a spirited Irish tune.

Two fine comic scenes dominate the play, both of them giving free rein to the comic energies of the widow. The park scene, in which she bursts in on Old Whittle just as he describes her "delicate reserve," allows for much physical humor as she prances, prates, sings, and abuses her servants in the crudest of Irish brogues, all the while displaying an utter lack of gentility. Interestingly, the widow, like other vacuous Garrick characters, sings at moments of greatest foolishness. The second scene is also bold farce, as the widow, in the guise of Lieutenant O'Neale, draws her sword, loosens her garters in order to duel effectively, and chases Old Whittle around the stage. As is characteristic with Garrick, the play is well crafted, with fast-paced action and fine comic dialogue. Whittle converses with Bates in a lighthearted moment:

> Whittle: You know, when I studied at Lincoln's Inn they used to call me Young Wisdom.
>
> Bates: And if they should now call you Old Folly it will be a much worse name. (1.1.148–51)

In addition, Garrick's characters are expertly drawn. His depiction of the widow emphasizes her intelligence, cunning, and basic goodness. Moreover, the two characters who are original Garrick creations, not drawn from Molière, Old Kecksy and Thomas, Old Whittle's footman, develop additional comedy out of improbable situations. Old Kecksy delights in his young wife, though she is five feet ten inches in height, defending his preference vigorously: "I hate your little shrimps; none of your lean meagre French frogs for me" (1.1.216–17). Thomas is comical in his refusal to wear a pigtail as his master wishes: "I could not help telling him that I was an Englishman born and had my prerogative as well as he, and that as long as I had breath in my body, I was for liberty and a straight head of hair" (1.1.112–15).

The London audiences were enthusiastic and the play was performed "By Command" of King George III on November 11, 1772. Hopkins, the prompter, noted in his Diary that "the King seem'd vastly pleas'd at the Farce." The play continued in its popularity well into the nineteenth century.

As in *Lilliput,* the satire is directed chiefly against the marriage of convenience, which is analyzed by Old Whittle's friend, Bates, thus: "The affair of marriage is in this country put upon the easiest footing. There is neither love or hate in the matter; necessity brings them together. They are united at first for their mutual convenience and separated ever after for their particular pleasures. Oh rare matrimony!" (1.1.55–59). Another object of satiric attack is the elderly man who becomes a rival of a young relative, a motif that had earlier appeared in *Miss in Her Teens, The Guardian,* and *The Clandestine Marriage.* Old Whittle, "on the debtor side sixty-five," is wholly ludicrous in his pursuit of his nephew's twenty-three-year-old fiancée: "He frisks and prances and runs about as if he had a new pair of legs. He has left off his brown camlet surtout, which he wore all summer, and now with his hat under his arm he goes open breasted, and he dresses and powders and smirks so, that you would take him for the mad Frenchman in Bedlam, something wrong in his upper story" (1.1.87–92).

Once again, Garrick deftly combined the outlines of an established work with his own farcical additions and mildly and happily satirized London.

**The Meeting of the Company; or, Bayes's Art of Acting** (1774). On the opening of the 1774 season Garrick wanted to celebrate the fact that Drury Lane had just been redecorated; thus he chose an Introductory Interlude in place of the more conventional Occasional Prologue. Characteristically, Garrick looked to any theater piece to reinforce and promulgate his theories on some aspect of good theater; in this case, he chose the art of acting. He explained his conception of the play to his good friend, Dr. John Hoadly: "I suppose yᵉ Manager has objections to Bayes's piece, the Poet to induce yᵉ Manager to Accept it, promises, if he will perform it, to make his Actors (the bad ones) equal to yᵉ best by a certain receipt he was master of, & had discover'd by long Study—the Manager agrees, the actors are call'd in, to be taught yᵉ great Secret—Bayes then gives them his Art of Acting—which will shew all yᵉ false manners of acting Tragedy & Comedy, wᶜʰ I have collected in about 30 or 40 comical Verses. . . ."[17]

Garrick thus created a theatrical setting in which he felt eminently comfortable, as well as one that had given him marked success in the past, notably in *A Peep Behind the Curtain.* As he had in *A Peep,* he used the rehearsal situation, which had long been a favorite device for satire on theater. This tradition in English drama dates from Beaumont and Fletcher's *Knight of the Burning Pestle* (1613) and received significant impetus from Buckingham's *Rehearsal* (1672), a favorite play during the eighteenth century and one in which Garrick had distinguished himself in the role of Bayes.

The cast of characters includes the Drury Lane prompter William Hopkins, and a Ballet Master, played by Grimaldi, ballet master at that theater. A number of actors, including Thomas Weston, played themselves, and the manager, called Patent, as in *A Peep Behind the Curtain,* represented Garrick. Garrick capitalized on the celebrity status that his actors had attained and the public affection in which they were held.

Weston emerges as the spokesman for the players and becomes the chief adversary to Bayes, the playwright, who comes "to prove to us all that there is nothing in acting tragedy or comedy" (115–16). Bayes addresses the assembled company as "patients" and instructs them in his cardinal principle: ". . . I will always oppose nature, that I am above her and despise her" (222–23). He details his position, advising them to eschew moderation on stage and to engage in distortion, to use grotesque costuming, and to cultivate affectation in speech. Bayes gives the players specific detailed advice for each of the major genres. For tragedy:

> Would you in tragedy extort applause,
> Distort *yourselves*—now rage, now start, now pause.
> Beat breast, roll eyes, stretch nose, up brows, down jaws.
> Then strut, stride, stare, goggle, bounce and bawl,
> And when you're out of breath, pant, drag and drawl.
>
> (310–14).

His advice to comic actors follows the same principles of exaggeration:

> Observe in comedy to frisk about.
> Never stand still. Jerk, work; fly in, fly out.
> Your faults conceal in flutter and in hurry,
> And with snip, snap, the poet's meaning worry,
> Like bullies hide your wants in bounce and vapor
> If memory fails, take snuff, laugh, curse and caper.
>                                                    (364–69).

In a moment reminiscent of *The Rehearsal* the players disappear, leaving the nonplussed Bayes to address the empty playhouse with his self-tested wisdom. He finally capitulates with a sigh: "Sic transit gloria mundi," and the play ends.

Through the figure of the self-important Bayes, Garrick humorously satirized all that was exaggerated in the acting of both comedy and tragedy. To make the situation more intimate and the instruction more palatable, he allowed jibes at himself and depicted both rivalry and camaraderie among his players. In *The Meeting of the Company* Garrick attained an effective blend of gossip, good humor, and orthodox thinking about the art of theatrical presentation. William Hopkins noted in his Diary: ". . . it is full of fine Satyr & an Excellent Lesson to all performers, it was receiv'd with very great Applause."

**Bon Ton; or High Life Above the Stairs** (1775).    It is especially appropriate that *Bon Ton* is Garrick's last original comedy, produced just fifteen months before his retirement.[18] He explains in the "Advertisement" to the play that it was brought out "as a token of regard" for Thomas King, the distinguished and popular Drury Lane comedian who had become a trusted long-time friend of Garrick and who had delighted audiences with his performances of the Fine Gentleman in *Lethe* and Lord Ogleby in *The Clandestine Marriage*. *Bon Ton* is Garrick's most finished play, peopled with both well-delineated characters and stock types, and propelled by sparkling dialogue. Moreover, the play is Garrick's fullest social statement on the false taste of eighteenth-century Londoners.

*Bon Ton* was introduced by a provocative Prologue written by George Colman in which the speaker canvasses representative citizens of London, seeking an answer to his question: "What is *Bon Ton?*" The respondents give clear, unequivocal answers: the buck sees it as freedom to pursue roisterous conduct; Madame Fussock, who mispronounces the term, views it as "the space 'twixt Saturday and Monday"; Miss sees it as "a constant trade/of rout, Festino, Ball and Masquerade!" Perhaps most ominous is the answer given by My Lord: for him it is a standard that allows for a certain code of conduct, by which "courtly friendship" forms a "treacherous league" to "seduce men's daughters, with their wives intrigue." Concluding this apt introduction to a comedy of manners, the speaker promises the audience "a sketch or two," like the prints of an eighteenth-century caricaturist.

The social arena which is the setting of the play is the home of Lord and Lady Minikin, a couple bound by their mutual disdain, and Miss Lucretia Tittup, Lady Minikin's niece. A visitor, Lady Minikin's cousin, Sir John Trotley, is astonished to find the household in a disarray of relationships: Lady Minikin is having an affair with her niece's fiancé, Colonel Tivy, while Lord Minikin is casting amorous glances at the niece, who concisely describes the situation: "My Lady Minikin likes him [Colonel Tivy], he likes my fortune; my Lord [Minikin] likes me, and I like my Lord" (1.1.105–06).

She looks forward to a fashionable marriage to Colonel Tivy, telling him, "Look'ee, Sir, I will command before marriage, and do what I please afterwards, or I have been well educated to very little purpose." When she leaves, the Colonel muses, with equal coldness: ". . . if I had the least affection for the girl, I should be damnably vexed at this.—but she has a fine fortune, and I must have her if I can" (1.1.160–65).

Sir John, however, finds that he cannot accept the situation with equanimity. He is astonished by the "dreadful change" that has occurred in London within the last twenty years. "I should not have known the place again, nor the people; all the signs that made so noble an appearance, are all taken down" (1.1.171–73). He is vexed by the informality of new hair styles for men: ". . . not a bob or tiewig to be seen," and by the behavior of the ladies of the streets, the "painted Jezebels." He is particularly concerned about the moral welfare of his niece, Miss Tittup, in this atmosphere: ". . . but what can be expected from the young women of these times, but sallow looks, wild schemes, saucy words, and loose morals!—They lie a-bed all day, sit up all night; if they are silent, they are gaming, and if they talk, 'tis either scandal or infidelity . . . O Tempora, O Mores!" (1.1.233–39).

Besides functioning as Garrick's rational commentator and communicating the author's view of London society, Sir John provides comedy in his earnest and total resistance to the dictates of fashion. The comedy provided by Lord Minikin and Tittup, however, is that of another sort: witty dialogue reminiscent of Restoration comedy. The young girl comes to Lord Minikin's room to warn him that his wife is suspicious of their relationship.

> Miss Tittup:   . . . she certainly has some mischief in her head.
>
> Lord Minikin:   No intentions, I hope, of being fond of me?
>
> Miss Tittup:   No, no, make yourself easy; she hates you most unalterably.
>
> Lord Minikin:   You have given me spirits again. (1.2.38–43)

The comedy changes in mid-scene as Sir John comes to Lord Minikin's room to discuss with him his concerns about his niece's behavior. Tittup is both embarrassed and frightened: ". . . if he sees me here alone with you, he'll rave like a madman; put me up the chimney,—anywhere" (1.2.80–81), and hides behind a chair. The physical comedy is extravagant as Lord Minikin is forced to turn the chair artfully in order to keep Miss Tittup concealed, as Sir John moves about the room. While Sir John earnestly speaks about the niece's dress and deportment, she peeps comically from behind the chair to exchange signs with Lord Minikin. During the conversation Lord Minikin tries to persuade Sir John that ". . . prudence is a very vulgar virtue, and so incompatible with our present ease and refinement," and he explains the fashionable attitude toward marriage:

Marriage is not now-a-days, an affair of inclination, but convenience; and they who marry for love, and such old-fashioned stuff, are to me as ridiculous as those that advertise for an agreeable companion in a post chaise. (1.2.156–59)

Angered, and vowing to return to the country the next day with Miss Tittup or disinherit her, Sir John leaves, only to return unexpectedly to find Lord Minikin on his knees before Miss Tittup, snatching her hand and kissing it.

Sir John's anger is compounded and the comedy is heightened when, upon visiting the apartment of Lady Minikin, whom he wants to invite to the country with him, he finds Tittup's fiancé, Colonel Tivy, in the same position in which Lord Minikin had been discovered: on his knees, kissing the lady's hand. "All pigs of the same sty!" is Sir John's indictment. Rejecting the challenge to a duel by Colonel Tivy, he renews his vow to return to the country.

Garrick artfully balances the serious moral views of Sir John with clever dialogue and extravagant physical comedy throughout the play. When Lord Minikin and Miss Tittup arrive home early from a masquerade to learn that Lady Minikin and Colonel Tivy also arrived early, Miss Tittup is forced to hide in a closet. Discovering that Lady Minikin's husband is home, Colonel Tivy dashes furiously to hide in the same closet but finds it locked and must take shelter behind a chimney-board. Husband and wife meet, exchange sarcastic pleasantries, and set out, each for his/her own apartment with a candle in hand. The stage directions have them "wipe their lips and exeunt ceremoniously." Each returns to the darkened stage within seconds to free his lover, but in the darkness Lord Minikin finds Lady Minikin, and the Colonel, Miss Tittup. The four are discovered by Sir John in his nightcap, who upon hearing the commotion has come to search for thieves.

The play ends quickly as Sir John, who has been the embodiment of reason throughout, addresses each of the lovers. Colonel Tivy is advised that, if Miss Tittup marries without his approval, she has no fortune, whereupon the Colonel makes a hasty exist. Lord Minikin learns he must meet his lawyers and creditors the next day and is told "that the dissipation of your fortune and morals, must be followed by years of parsimony and repentance." Finally, the ladies, who seem capable of rehabilitation, learn that they are to be whisked off to the country with Sir John, where they may regain their natural English constitutions.

Garrick's extraordinary success in *Bon Ton* may be credited to his ability to blend different elements of comedy and characterization. The clever dialogue and witty repartee of the members of Lord Minikin's household and Colonel Tivy are heightened by their alternation with elements of pure farce. The playwright had an expert and experienced view of time-tested comic devices. He effectively used hiding, whether behind chairs, boards, or in closets; characters groping in the dark, unaware of each other's presence; and mistaken identities. Moreover, in placing the voice of the rational commentator directly at the comic scene, the laughter-provoking incident is used to instruct as well as to entertain.

Garrick has also accomplished a masterful blend in characterization, deftly interweaving stock characters such as the servants Jes-

samy, Davy, and Gymp, with the more individualized Lord and Lady
Minikin, Miss Tittup, and Sir John Trotley. Miss Tittup is the most
original character in the group, witty, intelligent, and clever, somewhat suggestive of Millamant in Congreve's *The Way of the World*. Sir
John, in his championing of good sense and honesty, looks backward
to Aesop in *Lethe,* Bolgolam in *Lilliput,* Sir William in *The Male Coquette,* and Bates in *The Irish Widow.* In his fondness for country life
and his distrust of innovation, he is close to Mr. Hardcastle in Goldsmith's *She Stoops to Conquer.*

*Bon Ton* had announced its promise of satire in its title and it admirably met expectations. Primarily, the attack was leveled against
the indolent life style of men and ladies of quality and the moral las-
situde it cultivated. Specifically Garrick satirized marriages of convenience, as he had in *Lilliput* and *The Clandestine Marriage;* the
servile aping of French fashions, as he had in *The Irish Widow;* and
the newfound inordinate independence of servants.

The high-spirited comedy delighted audiences, and the play,
which has been called "one of the best miniature comedies in English
dramatic literature,"[19] retained its popularity on stage well into the
nineteenth century. *Bon Ton,* Garrick's last comedy, fittingly capped
thirty-five years of writing satiric and farcical works that were able to
elevate and entertain generations of London playgoers.

**The Clandestine Marriage** (1767). *The Clandestine Marriage,*
which David Garrick wrote in collaboration with George Colman,
was his only venture in formal co-authorship. The result was a play
that was acclaimed as the best comedy of the decade, retained its
popularity throughout the century, and has been called "one of
the few really excellent comedies that the eighteenth century produced."[20]

Garrick and Colman had been friends for years, and Garrick's magnetic charm was at least partly responsible for wooing Colman away
from the promising law career that his family had envisioned for him.
When Colman wrote his first play, *Polly Honeycombe* (1760), a short
farce satirizing the sentimentality of contemporary novels and the
busyness of the lending libraries which circulated them among sentimental young ladies, the literary antecedents of Sheridan's Lydia
Languish in *The Rivals* (1775), Garrick obliged Colman by lending
his name to the play so as not to antagonize Colman's family.

Colman turned to Garrick again the following year when he found
himself not quite satisfied with his new play, *The Jealous Wife.* He

wrote in the "Advertisement" that he sent the play to Garrick "in its first rude state" and benefited from the manager's advice "in many particulars, relating both to fable and characters." The collaboration of these two writers, each of whom maintained, up until this time, enormous respect and warmth for the other, was a natural outgrowth of a vital and productive friendship.

Arthur Murphy, a contemporary of the two, himself a practicing dramatist, tells us that they had devised their plan for writing *The Clandestine Marriage* before Garrick set out on his continental tour in 1763, each agreeing to a general plan, and each taking particular scenes and characters to develop. There are frequent references to the project in Garrick's correspondence, Garrick confessing his own frustration and pleading with Colman for some news of his progress. On April 11, 1764 Garrick wrote to Colman from Rome: "Speed y$^r$ Plow my d$^r$ friend, have you thought of the Clandestine M[arriage]? I am at it—I must desire you to write to me once more & direct a Mons$^r$ Mons$^r$ [*sic*] G____ Gentilhomme Anglais chez Monsieur Dutens a Turin, & I shall get it by hook or by crook."[21] He returns to the subject on November 10, 1764, writing to Colman from Paris: "Did you receive my Letter about our Comedy—I shall begin, the first moment I find my comic Ideas return to me, to divert myself w$^{th}$ Scribbling—say something to me upon that Subject—I have consider'd our 3 Acts, & with some little alterations they will do—I'll ensure them."[22]

The exact nature of the collaboration and the particular contributions of each writer have intrigued generations of scholars. Evidence indicates that Garrick conceived of the plot and provided material for the characterizations, including that for Lord Ogleby, the role he originally envisioned for himself.[23] Significantly, Colman generated the characterization of Sterling and the mercantile background for the Sterling family. The earliest draft of the play, then titled *The Sisters*, shows Garrick tailoring it to the capabilities of his company at Drury Lane. Indeed, instead of conventional character descriptions, the manuscript indicates the names of the actors and actresses for whom the roles were being written: Garrick is to play "an Old Beau"; Kitty Clive is to be cast as the aunt, later Mrs. Heidelberg; and Tom King is to play the role of "an old flattering Serv$^t$ of G's," later to be named Canton. Mrs. Bride is named as the elder sister and Mrs. Pope the younger sister; the name of Yates appears to play Garrick's brother, and that of O'Brien as the nephew, soon to be named Lovewell. Study of this manuscript copy of *The Sisters* tells us much about Garrick's creative process. Given the general outlines of the plot, he tailored it to the particular comic talents of specific performers. So canny was his pragmatic theatrical instinct and so successful the comic parts he wrote for his individual players that the performers playing the parts of Mrs. Heidelberg, Fanny, Lord Ogleby, and Trueman each chose *The Clandestine Marriage* for his/her benefit night.[24]

The action moves quickly about the central motif of the play, the discomfitures that devolve on Fanny Sterling, younger daughter of the prosperous merchant, and Lovewell, nephew of Lord Ogleby, because their four-month-old marriage has been kept secret. Although Fanny pleads with her husband to reveal the situation, he delays because he believes his poor financial condition will turn his mercenary father-in-law against him, unless his uncle, the charming superannuated Lord Ogleby, intercedes for him.

In the meantime, Betsy, Fanny's attractive older sister and a favorite of their domineering, wealthy, and outspoken aunt, Mrs. Heidelberg, has been betrothed to Sir John Melvil. When Sir John, however, meets his intended bride, his enthusiasm wanes; he finds himself more strongly attracted to the younger sister, Fanny. Unaware of the fact that she is already married, he obtains the permission of her merchant father to marry her, on condition that he accept a dowry of £50,000 rather than the £80,000 both men had agreed upon as Betsy's marriage settlement. All action is suspended when Mrs. Heidelberg expresses her anger at the slight dealt her minion, Betsy, and Melvil, like Lovewell, hopes for Lord Ogleby's assistance in his pursuit of Fanny. To add to the comedy, Lord Ogleby, a well-named devotee of the ladies, imagines that Fanny loves him and receives the astonished Sterling's consent for their marriage. A more comic moment is realized when a jubilant Lord Ogleby tells Fanny's husband, Lovewell, and her lovesick suitor, Sir John Melvil, of his good fortune and impending marriage.

The fifth-act scene set outside Fanny's apartment caps the action as Fanny and her husband meet inside, resolved to reveal their marriage to all on the following day. But a watch is set up by Betsy and Mrs. Heidelberg. The sister, having seen a man enter the apartment, believes it to be her fiancé, Sir John Melvil. Eventually, Sterling, Lord Ogleby, and Sir John appear, but, before Fanny can reveal the truth, she faints. After Lovewell comes forth, to the amazement and chagrin of all, and Fanny recovers sufficiently to reveal the fact of her marriage, Lord Ogleby intervenes with the enraged Sterling to bless the union. A general reconciliation is followed by familial congratulations, Lord Ogleby articulating the moral of the play:

Young ladies with minds like my Fanny's would startle at the very shadow of vice; and when they know to what uneasiness only an indiscretion has exposed her, her example, instead of encouraging, will rather serve to deter them. (5.2.370–74).

Much of the excellence of the play lies in the tightness of plot construction throughout and the relevance of each individual scene. Garrick and Colman created a fluidity of both action and setting, which lends plausibility to the situation, even though the reason for the secrecy of the marriage of Fanny and Lovewell is never adequately explained. The dialogue is fast-paced, moving the action along so that the viewer is not likely to pose questions. Two scenes in particular deserve examination because of their contribution to the dramatic line. The second scene of the first act is a masterpiece of careful dramatic architectonics as it portrays the pretentious and obnoxious behavior of Betsy Sterling and the overbearing ways of Mrs. Heidelberg. Failing to irritate Fanny with talk of her upcoming wedding to Sir John Melvil, Betsy berates her sister:

Pretty peevish soul! Oh, my dear grave, romantic sister! A perfect philosopher in petticoats! Love and a cottage, eh, Fanny! Ah, give me indifference and a coach and six!

To which Fanny replies:

And why not the coach and six without the indifference? But, pray, when is this happy marriage of yours to be celebrated? (1.2.17–21)

Betsy reveals that her obnoxious behavior extends beyond the family when, she admits that in shopping for her wedding attire, she "sat above an hour in the parlor behind the shop consulting Lady Lutestring about gold and silver stuffs on purpose to mortify her" (1.2.45–47). She disdains this woman simply because she is a city-knight's lady and thus not one of the landed nobility.

The scene is important, too, in introducing the gusty, loquacious, and outspoken Mrs. Heidelberg who enters, detailing a long list of domestic preparations to be made in advance of the visit that evening

of Lord Ogleby and Sir John, Betsy's fiancé. Although she is inti-
mately concerned with Betsy's romantic life, she has little concern for
Fanny, sending her away in tears, with the rebuff:

Bless me, why, your face is as pale and black and yellow—of fifty colors, I
pertest. And then you have drest yourself as loose and as big—I declare
there is not such a thing to be seen now as a young woman with a fine waist.
(1.2.127–30).

Mrs. Heidelberg mistakenly attributes Fanny's tears to her romantic
interest in Lovewell:

She is gone away in tears—absolutely crying, I vow and pertest. This ridiculous love; we must put a stop to it. It makes a perfect nataral of the girl.
(1.2.134–36)

In addition to revealing the characters of the ladies, the scene deftly
prepares the audience for the imminent appearance of Lord Ogleby,
about whom much of the comedy revolves.

The play's concluding scene, described earlier, is a theatrical tour
de force. The imperious Mrs. Heidelberg and her simpering niece,
Betsy, are counterpointed against the antics of the half-drunk Brush,
Sir Ogleby's valet, who flirts with the frightened chambermaid. The
maid is sent to summon Sterling to the site of the supposed debauch-
ery and, from this point on, the comedy develops around the carefully
timed entrances and exits of several characters. Fanny's maid, Betty,
comes out of her mistress's room, calmly locks the door, and puts the
key into her pocket. Sterling enters the scene, quickly followed by
his sister, Mrs. Heidelberg, who had absented herself briefly in order
to obtain a new headdress so that she might look her best in the middle of the night. Canton, Lord Ogleby's Swiss gentleman, arrives in
nightgown and slippers, but exits quickly as Lord Ogleby rings for
him. Sterling exits to obtain lights for Sergeant Flower and Traverse,
the attorneys, who reenter with him. Finally, Lord Ogleby, in his
*robe de chambre* and nightcap, enters and attempts to entice Fanny
"from her pillow with a whisper through the keyhole." The excitement of this concatenation of events tells on Betsy, who asks excit-
edly, "Now what will they do? My heart will beat thro' my bosom."
When Betty agrees to open the door, Lord Ogleby summons Sir John
Melvil from the bedroom "to appear and answer to high crimes and
misdemeanors." Sir John promptly enters from the other side! Lord

Ogleby maintains his amiability, teasing Betsy and Mrs. Heidelberg: "Upon my word, ladies, if you have often these frolics it would be really entertaining to pass a whole summer with you" (5.2.300–301). Finally, Fanny and Lovewell appear and reconciliations are urged by Lord Ogleby.

In addition to such masterful scene construction and the plausibility of actions therein depicted, Garrick relied on memorable characterization for the success of the play. Indeed, his subtle blending of different kinds of characters accounts for much of the comic thrust of the play. Lord Ogleby, the character Garrick originally intended to play, is the drama's moving force. The actor, Thomas Davies, described Garrick's amiable rake thus:

The part of Lord Ogleby is a finished portrait: an enervated debauchée, affecting all the warmth and gaiety of youth, and making love to a fine young lady, is a character, if not odious, at least contemptible; but the skillful hand of the author, by giving him humane and generous principles, has not only saved him from our hatred, but has dignified him with a degree of approbation which the man of a benevolent mind will always be sure to obtain.

Davies indicates the uniqueness of the character, noting that "the part is happily discriminated from any other libertine of rank."[25] Modern criticism is equally enthusiastic: "Lord Ogleby is a kind of summary of Garrick's comic talents—of the simple-minded Abel Drugger, the coxcomb Bayes, Lord Chalkstone the dandy, even drunken Sir John Brute."[26] Similarly, Mrs. Heidelberg has a predecessor in the self-important, garrulous Mrs. Riot of *Lethe*. Even the minor characters are well chiseled: Canton, Lord Ogleby's Swiss gentleman, and Betty, the cool-headed servant of Fanny, act with energy and independence, thus contributing significantly to the play. Both are well-developed type characters from the established comic tradition: Canton, nicknamed "Cant" by Ogleby, is the world-wise valet-confidante of French farce and Betty is the perky soubrette.

Garrick created a pair of lovers, Fanny and Lovewell, to satirize the characters of sentimental comedy with which his irritation was steadily growing. His letter of April 30, 1770 to the Reverend Charles Jenner articulates his preference for a more robust "Comedy of Character": ". . . one calculated to make an Audience Laugh than cry— the *Comedie Larmoyante* is getting too Much ground upon Us, & if those who can write the better species of y$^e$ Comic drama don't make a Stand for y$^e$ Genuine Comedy & vis comica the Stage in a few years will be (as Hamlet says) like Niobe all tears—."[27]

The aptly named Lovewell and Fanny remain true to each other in their halcyon love, despite the turmoil about them, as a pair of sentimental lovers should. Fanny, ever lachrymose, finds it difficult to deal with the problems that have resulted from the secrecy of her marriage: she blushes as Betty alludes to her early pregnancy, breaks into tears when her aunt comments on her appearance, blushes on addressing Lord Ogleby to ask his help, weeps on hearing his addresses of love, and faints on coming out of the bedroom into the gallery to meet the assembled crowd. A predecessor of Sheridan's Lydia Languish in *The Rivals,* Fanny is overly genteel and overrefined, and thus the object of Garrick's satirical thrust.

The supporting characters, the mercenary Sterling who boasts to Lord Ogleby, "It has just cost me a hundred and fifty pounds to put my ruins in thorough repair"; Fanny's aunt, Mrs. Heidelberg, whose only concern is for "people of qualaty"; and her scheming sister Betsy, who believes herself "born to move in the sphere of the great world," are all meant to satirize the pretentiousness and vulgarity of the newly rich middle class in London. Marriages of convenience are also satirized through scheming Betsy and her pragmatic aunt. Sergeant Flower and his legal assistants, Traverse and Trueman, in their circuitous reasoning and their overuse of Latin tag-words, poke good-natured fun at the legal profession.

The success of the play was immediate and emphatic. When first performed, it played to enthusiastic audiences for thirteen consecutive nights and, during its second season, topped all other plays (except the Christmas play, *Cymon*) in number of performances and box-office receipts. The play was widely sold in its printed form, going through three editions in the first three weeks. Its popularity grew with each performance and it was acted well into the nineteenth century.

*The Clandestine Marriage,* Garrick's only formal venture in co-authorship, possessed many of the excellences of his singly written comedies and farces, and, like them, it both entertained and educated its enthusiastic audiences.

## Chapter Three

# The Playwright as Taste-Maker: The Musical Plays

Although Garrick had no formal musical training, he was a sensitive and intelligent listener who readily acknowledged the impact of music in the playhouse. Moreover, he recognized that music in the theater had been a part of the English dramatic tradition from medieval times to his own. In addition, as theatrical entrepreneur, he noted the success of musical productions on the rival stages of Covent Garden and the King's Opera House, and he attempted to draw his share of the music-loving public to Drury Lane.

Within the first decade of his management of Drury Lane, Garrick sought to elevate the status of serious music in his playhouse by commissioning John Christopher Smith, a pupil of Handel and successful composer in his own right, to write the music for *The Fairies* (1775), an operatic adaptation of *A Midsummer Night's Dream,* and for an operatic version of *The Tempest* (1756). Three years later, upon the departure of his clever pantomimist, Henry Woodward, to Dublin, and in response to the increasing public taste for plays that incorporated much music, Garrick decided to write a pantomime himself, *Harlequin's Invasion.* His success in integrating music into the play encouraged him to continue to write plays in which music was a significant and necessary element. Writing musical plays became for Garrick one of his most exciting professional challenges and one of his chief playwriting interests in the 1760s and 1770s.

After adapting the Shakespearean works into operas, Garrick wrote ten original musical plays which lend themselves to the following classification: (a) four Christmas plays, *Harlequin's Invasion* (1759); *The Enchanter* (1760); *Cymon* (1767); and *A Christmas Tale* (1773); (b) two operatic works incorporating sophisticated music by eminent composers, *A Peep Behind the Curtain* (1767) and *May Day* (1775); (c) two plays written to commemorate events of contemporary interest,

*The Jubilee* (1769) and *The Institution of the Garter* (1771); and (d) two
extremely short pieces, an interlude, *Linco's Travels* (1767), and a musical prelude, *The Theatrical Candidates* (1775).

## Operatic Adaptations of Shakespeare

*The Fairies* (1755).   In 1755 Garrick attempted to join the two
great theatrical forces of the moment: the burgeoning love of authentic Shakespearean plays, as indicated by his great success in adapting
*Macbeth* in 1744 and *Romeo and Juliet* in 1748, and the demand of
audiences for music in the playhouse, as evidenced by the popularity
of musical productions at Covent Garden and at the King's Opera
House. The natural result of such a union seemed to be a serious English opera based on Shakespeare.

Aware of the characteristic objections of the Englishman to Italian
opera and aware of the failure of native composers and librettists before him to produce a successful native opera, Garrick set out to write
one with the aid of the composer, John Christopher Smith. In the
Prologue Garrick observes with heavy irony:

> Excuse us first for foolishly supposing
> Your countryman could please you in composing;
> An op'ra too!—played by an English band,
> Wrote in a language which you understand—.

Realizing that one of the most frequently voiced objections to Italian
opera was that the audience did not understand the plot, he
continues:

> This awkward drama—(I confess th'offence)
> Is guilty too, of poetry and sense.

Nevertheless, he says, the young playwright, "Struck with the wonders of his master's art," will attempt to render a musical based on
Shakespeare.

Garrick's intent was to fashion a musical inspired by Shakespeare,
not to recast a Shakespearean play in operatic form. Therefore, he
confined himself to the magical scenes of *A Midsummer Night's Dream*
and the adventures of the two pairs of lovers, Hermia and Lysander,
and Helena and Demetrius. In so doing, he used only about twenty
percent of the lines from the play. His approach to the addition and

revision of lines was that of a "play doctor." When the exigencies of stage business, or the need for clarity, or the use of transitional lines was necessary, he intervened as adapter. Otherwise, he used the Shakespearean lines. As George C.D. Odell has remarked, "A good deal of Shakespeare's poetry is retained intact . . . Garrick left in their original purity the Shakespearean verses he used—he merely omitted or put in—but in either case it was solid blocks that went or stayed."[1]

Garrick did not feel the same compunction for purity when he supplied the songs for Smith to set. Only eleven of the twenty-eight are taken from Shakespeare and only four of these eleven originate in *A Midsummer Night's Dream.* Three of the eleven are spoken lines in the original Shakespearean play, here set to music. The remaining four are taken from other Shakespearean plays, including *The Tempest, Much Ado About Nothing, King Henry V,* and *Love's Labor's Lost.*

Where Garrick found it impossible to use the original source or adapt Shakespearean songs, he appropriated poetry from esteemed English figures such as John Milton, Edmund Waller, John Dryden, James Hammond, and George Granville, Lord Lansdowne, and had Smith set them to music. Despite their eclectic origins, the songs are both well balanced and dramatically effective.

In the third act, immediately preceding Oberon's charming of Demetrius, which causes him to fall in love with Helena, the distraught Hermia, grieving for Lysander, sings, "How calm's the sky, how undisturbed the deep!"—an original song by Garrick. The next song, occurring soon after, is sung by Oberon, as he anoints Demetrius's eyes, "Flower of this Purple Dye." It directs Demetrius's action on awakening and is the original Shakespearean song. In the next scene Lysander, who has been charmed by Puck in error, awakens to pay his addresses to Helena in the song, "Do Not Call It Sin in Me," which are Dumain's lines in *Love's Labor's Lost.* Helena's next song, "Since Hermia Neglects Me," is an original composition by Garrick. This is followed by Lysander's "Come Pride, Love-disdaining," in which, still under Puck's spell, he proclaims his love for Helena. This is another original composition of Garrick. When Oberon appears in the next scene, he sings "Sigh No More, Ladies, Sigh No More," lines appropriated from Balthasar in *Much Ado About Nothing.*

Garrick's achievement in the use, appropriation, and composition of songs is remarkable in that he has preserved dramatic continuity by choosing pre-existent material that advances his plot line clearly and economically. Moreover, in carefully restricting his literary sources he has managed to sustain the stately language and serious tone of the original Shakespearean play.

Garrick's careful blending of elements of Shakespeare's play with adroit staging of the magical scenes and the use of Smith's stately post-Handelian music created a work that the first-night audience responded to with "very great applause," according to prompter, Richard Cross. In addition to his usual Drury Lane company, Garrick had cast two celebrated Italian singers from the King's Opera House, Signor Guadagni as Lysander and Signora Passerini as Hermia, in recognition of the technical sophistication of Smith's music.[2] This move gave the play "great additional service," according to actor Tate Wilkinson.[3]

Garrick had achieved a critical success in writing *The Fairies,* but he had not created a theatrical staple. The play appealed to the exalted tastes for music and poetry of some members of the audience, but it failed to capture the robust enthusiasm of the broader audience. It played for eleven performances, giving Garrick some hope for the possibilities of such composition, but the practical manager had to withdraw the play from the permanent repertory of Drury Lane in favor of heartier theatrical fare.

*The Tempest* (1756).    The vehicle to which Garrick instinctively turned next was the enormously popular Restoration adaptation of Shakespeare's *Tempest,* originally co-authored by John Dryden and William Davenant in 1670, and further adapted in 1674 by Thomas Shadwell.

The Dryden-Davenant adaptation of the *Tempest* is characterized by a balancing of characters. Hippolito, a man who has never seen a woman, is created as a counterpart to Shakespeare's Miranda "that by this means those two Characters of Innocence and Love might the more illustrate and commend each other," according to the Preface to the 1670 edition. Moreover, Caliban is given an equally unpleasant sister, Sycorax; Ariel has a lover, Milcha, and Miranda obtains a sister, Dorinda. As one modern critic has noted, "Everything in this play goes in couples."[4] Whatever portion of Shakespeare's text accommodates the Dryden-Davenant scheme is virtually untouched, but the different dramatis personae and the different aims and emphases of the playwrights result in a play that is only remotely similar to Shakespeare's comedy.

Shadwell's later alteration of *The Tempest* did not make substantial changes in the text, but rather added to its spectacular effects of music and machinery. He added music composed by the leading contemporary composers, both English and continental: J. Hart, Giovanni Battista Draghi, Matthew Locke, John Banister, Pelham Humphrey, and Pietro Reggio, and he inserted dances created by Draghi. Shadwell also contributed elaborate scenic effects, writing explicit directions: ". . . when the Ship is sinking, the whole House is darken'd, and a shower of Fire falls upon 'em. This is accompanied with Lightning, and several Claps of Thunder, to the end of the Storm."

Although the Dryden-Davenant-Shadwell adaptation has been damned by later critics, the enthusiasm of Restoration and early eighteenth-century audiences was almost boundless. By mid-century, however, its popularity had begun to wane, giving Garrick his opportunity to attempt a more authentic presentation of Shakespeare's text, supported by serious and stately music. Garrick decided on an operatic *Tempest,* stressing those elements in the play that lent themselves to musical presentation. Once again he engaged John Christopher Smith to compose the score.

In a characteristic move, Garrick preceded his opera with a 140-line dialogue between two aptly named gentlemen, Wormwood and Heartly. Wormwood opposes the musical treatment of great writers on stage, complaining "that this frittering and sol-fa-ing our best poets is a damned thing." Heartly, a devotee of music, listens to his many complaints before reciting Lorenzo's lines from the *Merchant of Venice,* "The man that has not music in himself," concluding "Let no such man be trusted." He then appeals to Wormwood's patriotic instincts as an Englishman before making a plea for the encouragement of native composers. Heartly concludes the dialogue with the advice: ". . . let not our musical brethren be cast off because fashion, caprice, or manners too refined may have given you prejudices against 'em. Music is the young sister of poetry and can boast her charms and accomplishments." Garrick thus anticipated the objections that he believed would be made to his musical *Tempest* and gave himself the opportunity to answer them.

For the opera itself, he provides the following argument: because of Prospero's raising a tempest, Alonso, King of Naples; his brother, Sebastian; Anthonio, the usurping Duke of Milan; and Ferdinand, Alonso's son, are shipwrecked on the island controlled by Prospero. In the meantime Prospero arranges that Ferdinand, Alonso's son who is thought to be lost by his father, meet Prospero's daughter, Miranda. As Prospero expects, the young people fall in love and he ar-

CARNEGIE LIBRARY
LIVINGSTONE COLLEGE
SALISBURY, N. C. 28144

ranges to bring all the principals together at his cave where the truth
is revealed about Ferdinand's survival. Confronted by this discovery,
Anthonio agrees to restore Prospero to his rightful place as Duke and
the betrothal of Miranda and Ferdinand follows in due course.

Although Garrick uses much of the Shakespearean text, he also
borrows both text and music from the Dryden-Davenant-Shadwell
*Tempest* and takes one song from Dryden's *Tyrannic Love*. The opera
ends with a duet between Ferdinand and Miranda, "Love, Gentle
Love, Now Fill My Breast." In all, Garrick incorporated thirty-two
songs into his dramatic text, only three of them from Shakespeare.
Smith's score was varied and interesting, including an accompanied recitative and a hornpipe for wind instruments alone. Comparing the
music of *The Tempest* with what Smith had composed for *The Fairies*,
Roger Fiske notes: "The music [of *The Tempest*] . . . is superior. It is
somewhat lighter in style, and it looks as though Garrick tried to
persuade Smith to find a more British type of melody and accompan-
iment. Handelian fingerprints still abound, but the songs are shorter
and more obviously tuneful. . . ."[5]

Although *The Tempest* found a receptive first-night audience, the
enthusiasm subsided quickly. Moreover, *The Tempest* received a heavy
critical attack. Tate Wilkinson said that "it was dreadfully heavy,"[6]
and Arthur Murphy lamented the fact that the play had been allowed
"to dwindle into an opera."[7] Theophilus Cibber attacked Garrick vigorously, claiming that *The Tempest* had been "castrated into an
opera."[8]

*The Tempest* was performed only six times. Garrick's attempt to
combine the poetry of Shakespeare with the graces of her "young sister" had failed unequivocally. Hereafter, his attempts to bring Shakespeare to the eighteenth-century stage were unaccompanied by
ancillary arts. From this point on, his ideal was to come as close as
possible to restoring the full, authentic Shakespearean text of the
plays.

## Christmas Entertainments

*Harlequin's Invasion* (1759). *Harlequin's Invasion*, a pantomime, was the first of Garrick's four theater pieces written specifically for presentation during the Christmas season, when by tradition
the English public had come to expect light, fantastic entertainment,
often decorated by processions, dances, pantomimes, and spectacle.

The justification for the extravaganza was presumably in the moral, which was often as simple as the production was lavish.

Pantomime, a popular form of Christmas entertainment in the English theater, had been introduced into England early in the century by John Weaver, a Drury Lane dancing master, and had been developed and popularized by John Rich, first, manager of Lincoln's Inn Fields and, later, builder of Covent Garden and manager of that theater from 1732 to 1761. Though completely illiterate and wholly ineffectual in acting conventional parts, Rich was an excellent actor in dumb show and attained unparalleled success in the pantomime, playing Harlequin under the name of Lun.

Thomas Davies describes his contribution: "Rich created a species of dramatic composition unknown to this, and, I believe, to any other country, which he called Pantomime. It consisted of two parts, one serious, the other comic; by the help of gay scenes, fine habits, grand dances, appropriate music, and other decorations, he exhibited a story from 'Ovid's Metamorphosis,' or some other fabulous history. Between the pauses of the acts he interwove a comic fable, consisting chiefly of the courtship of Harlequin and Columbine, with a variety of surprising adventures and tricks, which were produced by the magic wand of Harlequin; such as the sudden transformation of palaces and temples to huts and cottages; of men and women into wheelbarrows and joint stools; of trees turned to houses; colonnades to beds of tulips; and mechanic shops into serpents and ostriches."[9]

As manager of Covent Garden, Rich loomed as a formidable rival to David Garrick, for every one of his pantomimes was a great success and he was universally praised for his expertise in silent, but expressive action and for the good taste and sumptuousness of his spectacular entertainments. In 1750 Garrick had begun to present pantomimes successfully at Drury Lane, having six of them written and enacted by the comedian, Henry Woodward, who came to be known as Lun, Jr.

Garrick was drawn to write his own pantomime as much by his desire to experiment with the form, as to fill the void created when Woodward departed for Dublin in 1758. Garrick's pantomime, though developed from Rich's pattern, was characteristically innovative. Contrary to the pantomime tradition, Garrick created a speaking harlequin, and Frenchified him as a foolish Monsieur Harlequin, exploiting the strong feelings that were then running against France, an adversary in the Seven Years War. In addition, he wrote into the play William Boyce's spirited and patriotic sea song, "Heart of Oak." Finally, he peopled the work with rustics which allowed him the opportunity to satirize domineering wives, milquetoast husbands, and fickle young girls.

Action moves quickly in this bustling little play as Mercury, accompanied by two heralds, two trumpets, drum and fife, and chorus, enters Charing Cross, that is, the realm of Dramatica, to warn the townspeople of an imminent invasion by M. Harlequin. The challenge is sounded:

> Let the light troops of Comedy march to attack him,
> And Tragedy whet all her daggers to hack him.
> Let all hands and hearts do their utmost endeavor.
> Sound trumpet, beat drum, King Shakespear forever.
>                                                    (1.1.46–49)

Responding to this call, shrewish Mrs. Snip sends her husband, the meek tailor Joe Snip, as her champion to return with the head of Harlequin. But he is easily duped by Harlequin, who, disguised as Snip's neighbor Taffy, beguiles the tailor into entering a cave, whereupon Bounce and Gasconade, similarly fooled by Harlequin into believing that Joe Snip in armor is the actual Harlequin, cut off Joe's head. The crafty Harlequin then, assuming Snip's appearance, has Forge deliver Snip's head to his home, where his daughter Dolly has already broken off with her suitor, Abram, convinced that she will soon be a grand lady, the daughter of the town hero.

A crowd-pleasing scene follows in which Harlequin, now captured, is brought before three fussy justices, who sentence him to a whipping for claiming that he has the power to decapitate them and then restore their heads. Challenged, Harlequin practices a comic decapitation: the wigs of the three justices fly off the moment before they are transformed into three old women. In the meantime Bounce and Gasconade are released from prison, where they have been awaiting execution, when Joe Snip appears alive and intact.

When Harlequin, now disguised as a friar, is recognized by the rustics, he, as a diversionary tactic, first sinks the prison, then restores it. Although Harlequin escapes, he is captured by Mercury, Jove's emissary, and returned to the group. There he is forced by Mercury to view his fate: a huge transparency "representing the powers of pantomime going to attack Mount Parnassus. A storm comes on, destroys the fleet," and Mercury solemnly delivers Jove's decree to Harlequin:

> Wait on the muses' train like fools of yore,
> Beware encroachment and invade no more.
>
> (3.2.113–14)

The spectacle is enlarged as Shakespeare appears on stage and Harlequin sinks. A chorus of many of Shakespeare's characters enters, accompanied by the three Graces who dance to the Finale. At the end of the second stanza several fairies and genii enter, the fairies dancing to the music. The earlier appeal to patriotism expands to an appeal to good literary taste in the final stanza:

> Ye Britons may fancy ne'er lead you astray,
> Nor e'er through your senses your reason betray.
> By your love to the Bard may your wisdom be known,
> Nor injure his fame to the loss of your own.
>
> (3.2.131–34)

Figure dancers who have come on stage during the final stanza join in the Grand Dance while the Chorus is sung and repeated. The stage is filled to overflowing, the music resounds, and the good feelings of patriotism and literary pride are invoked in Garrick's audience, contributing to the success of the play.[10]

Garrick delighted the audience by the use of transparencies, the work of Domenico Angelo, whom the playwright approached in his search for "a scene, such as would be likely to attract by its novelty." Eighteenth-century practice was to paint scenery in opaque colors on canvas. In using a transparency, the back scene is painted on linen or calico in transparent colors. When viewed from the front with normal front lighting, the back scene looks like all others; but, if it is lighted from behind, the painting on the front of the fabric either fades or is given dimension by additional painting on the back. In this way it is possible to change the entire effect, from that of a normal building, for example, to that of a building burning. Years later Henry Angelo recalled his father's inventiveness in designing the transparencies:

He caused screens to be placed diagonally which were covered with scarlet, crimson, and bright blue moreen, which, having a powerful light before them, but turning them towards the scenes, reflected these various colours alternately, with a success that astonished and delighted the audience. Indeed, the whole stage appeared on fire.[11]

The transparencies, used in the scenes in which Harlequin sinks the prison and restores it and in the view of the powers of Pantomime about to attack Parnassus, appealed to the audience's ever-increasing love of spectacle. The spectacle was enhanced by Garrick's wise choice of music in the songs of Michael Arne and Theodore Aylward, in addition to the celebrated "Heart of Oak" by Boyce.

*Harlequin's Invasion* delighted its first-night audience on December 31, 1759 and remained popular in the Drury Lane repertory. Thomas King, the veteran comedian who won plaudits as Harlequin, requested the pantomime often on benefit nights, knowing it would draw an audience.

In committing himself to pantomime Garrick had done so with style and grace, and from that date onwards, pantomimes were among the most popular Christmas entertainments at Drury Lane.

*The Enchanter* (1760).   In preparing his Christmas diversion for 1760 Garrick capitalized on two fast-growing trends: the English fascination with the Eastern tale and the increasing popularity of light, entertaining music. The delight in Eastern personalities and often complicated intrigue plots is evident in both dramatic and nondramatic literature of the period. The enthusiastic reception of Montesquieu's *Persian Letters* had crystallized an interest in the East that had been evident since the popularity of heroic plays during the post-Restoration period. The Eastern tale offered Garrick the exotic land to which he could transport his Drury Lane holiday audience, and its remoteness offered him the possibility of dramatizing a good-versus-evil tale in its barest outlines without seeming overly didactic.

Garrick engaged John Christopher Smith, who had earlier set the music for *The Fairies* (1756) and *The Tempest* (1756), to produce the music for this play. The combining of Garrick's Eastern tale and Smith's music resulted in a two-act miniature opera, incorporating the pageantry and scenic effects that audiences had come to expect from that musical form.

The lovely Zaida, who is pledged to Zoreb, is carried off by the sinister magician, Moroc, to his castle, where he hopes to entice her into accepting him. He is astonished to learn that Zaida will remain faithful to Zoreb:

What uncommon mold
Impressed thy mind, that pleasure, power, nor gold
Can soften or allure it.

(1.2.35–37)

Defeated, he gives his magic wand to his servant Kaliel, to use what enchantments are necessary to win the maiden, but Kaliel, too, is unsuccessful. Enraged and vengeful, Moroc then returns, determined to convince Zaida that her lover is dead and that constancy is futile. To the strains of a dead march he conjures up a tomb in which Zoreb is lying. In a mad passion Zaida attempts to stab herself, and, in the ensuing scuffle in which Moroc tries to prevent her action, he drops his magic wand. This is seized by the servant, Kaliel, who now assumes supremacy over his master, thus ending his "guilty reign." The stage directions note that "While the symphony is playing, Zoreb rises gradually from the tomb" and "Looks rapturous on Zaida." The lovers engage in a joyous duet, "No Power Could Divide Us, No Terror Dismay," and are joined by shepherds and shepherdesses who, with Kaliel, enter into the singing. The play ends with the final dance of all characters on stage.

Attempting to make his opera appealing to the large theatergoing public, Garrick attacked, in the "Advertisement" to the play, the traditional operatic object of scorn among Englishmen, the recitative. "As the recitative commonly appears the most tedious part of the musical entertainment, the writer of the following little piece has avoided it as much as possible; and has endeavored to carry on what fable there is, chiefly by the songs." The score shows a series of rather simple, tuneful songs, Smith only once using the *da capo* form of his master, Handel. He scored the songs for the large theater orchestra which included recorders, flutes, horns, trumpets, timpani, and strings.

Garrick attained remarkable success in structuring this little play as an opera, that is, in carrying the dramatic line primarily by music. For instance, the first air, "I burn! I burn!" serves the traditional first-act expository function in revealing Moroc's insatiable desire for Zaida:

Where e'er I turn
Each object feeds my flame;

(1.1.4–5)

This in turn prepares for Kaliel's air, in which he assures his master that he has tried his full powers of persuasion on Zaida to no success. Moroc's commands to the spirits of the underworld to use enchantment to accomplish his ends is also rendered in an air.

Merrill Knapp has commented on the dramatic nature of the music, not only in the dead march, which is reminiscent of Handel's *Saul,* but also in Smith's lighter, more original music. Zaida's plaintive air, sung as she wanders unhappily in the Enchanter's garden:

> Intruder sleep! In vain you try
> To hush my breast and close my eye;
> (1.4.54–55)

is an arioso with "a graceful melody." On the other hand, Zaida's reaction to seeing Zoreb lying in his tomb is well expressed in the air, "Back to Your Source, Weak Foolish Tears," a conventional Italian rage aria "of rapid, rushing strings," and "a jagged vocal line that goes up two octaves." Yet another mood is conveyed in the finale in which the shepherds and shepherdesses join the lovers in a typical pastoral set in 6/8 time in which each singer joins in the "catchy melody."[12]

*The Enchanter* was first presented on December 13, 1760 and was, according to Hopkins, "very well received." Garrick's first venture in the world of fantasy was successful and the playwright, more conscious than ever of the power of well-chosen music to heighten characterization, communicate mood, and function integrally in the plot, began to move confidently in the realm of musical drama.

*Cymon* (1767). *Cymon,* the dramatic romance Garrick devised from Dryden's verse fable of *Cymon and Iphigenia,* was another Christmas treat created for the holiday season, containing a variety of enticing ingredients: music, dance, spectacle, an exotic setting, and the expected moral. Garrick provided these elements in abundance and his audience, both those in the pit and in the boxes, according to Horace Walpole, responded enthusiastically.[13]

Urganda, an Arcadian enchantress, has abducted Cymon, a foolish prince whom she loves. For Cymon, who does not return her feelings, she spurns Merlin who loves her, inciting him to a revengeful curse: "Cymon's cure shall be Urganda's wound." Hopeful that a change of scene for Cymon might stimulate his feelings for her, Urganda finally grants the unhappy prince his freedom. Upon his promise that he will return to her soon, she gives him an enchanted nosegay to increase his passion for her. But through Merlin's power, Cymon falls wholly in love with Sylvia, a beautiful young shepherdess whom he has found sleeping in the countryside. Sylvia also gives him a nosegay as a pledge of her love. When Urganda, to whom he returns with a new awareness, learns this, she is possessed of a "racking jealousy" and lays her sinister plans for Sylvia: "I will make her more wretched than any of her sex—except myself."

Urganda has Cymon closely watched, but Merlin, still stung by jealousy and anger, uses all his powers to protect the lovers. The governor, Dorus, his deputy, Linco, and two shepherds who are former suitors of Sylvia, are all pressed into action upon Urganda's orders, but Merlin, true to his word, protects Cymon and Sylvia, and tells Urganda that it is he who has safeguarded them through all her plots. Urganda accepts Merlin's pronouncement that, in punishment for her wicked ways, she must abdicate the throne of Arcadia. Merlin then articulates Garrick's moral, explaining the rightness of things: "Falsehood is punished, virtue rewarded, and Arcadia is restored to peace, pleasure, and innocence."

The playwright follows his "message" with a description of the procession, the most spectacular moment of the play:

Enter the procession of knights of the different orders of Chivalry, with Enchanters, &c., who range themselves round the amphitheatre, followed by Cymon, Sylvia, and Merlin, who are brought in triumph drawn by Loves, preceded by Cupid and Hymen, walking arm and arm. Then enter the Arcadian shepherds, with Dorus and Linco at their head, Damon and Dorilas with their shepherdesses &c.

The play ends with a merry song in which all join, followed by a dance of Arcadian shepherds and shepherdesses.

Garrick spared no effort in concocting a magnificent spectacle in his fairytale kingdom. From his opening scene, the palace of Urganda, the scene is changed to "a magnificent garden" upon the wave of Urganda's wand, and later to "a rural prospect," to introduce the two shepherdesses and Linco, Dorus's merry deputy. The garden episode, both spectacular and clearly comic, consists of one of the "flyings" in which Cupid and his followers descend, Cupid rendering the words of a comic air, "Oh, why will you call me again, . . . The powers of a god/ Cannot quicken this clod" (1.1.188–91). Cupid and his followers then engage in a dance, the charm of which is apparently lost on the dull-witted Cymon, who eventually falls asleep.

Transformations were used to effect the fourth-act scene in which the wicked Urganda "waves her wand and the castle vanishes." The first Demon of Revenge then arises through the front trap, while an underground chorus of furies chant their support: "We come, we come, we come." Then they "arise and perform their rites."

Another transformation is called for when Sylvia in captivity is brought before Urganda in the palace. Urganda "waves her wand, and the scene changes to the black rocks." When the shepherdess refuses to sink before Urganda in fear, asserting, "While I have Cymon in my heart, I bear a charm about me to scorn your power or, what is more, your cruelty" (5.1.95–96), Urganda "waves her wand and the Black Tower appears." A burst of thunder issues, and a transformation shows the tower and rocks giving way to a "magnificent amphitheatre." Appearing before Urganda, who is frozen in terror, Merlin grimly reminds her of his earlier curse, "And Cymon's cure shall be Urganda's wound," before banishing her.

The puzzlement that modern critics have expressed about the great popularity of *Cymon*[14] is due to their failure to appreciate the musical component of the play which was consciously written to enhance its dramatic value. Garrick arranged on August 22, 1766 to have the music written by Michael Arne, who had composed the music for John Hawkesworth's *Edgar and Emmeline* (1761) and had contributed songs to *A Fairy Tale* (1763) and *Almena* (1764). Arne produced a score that is remarkable for its diversity. It included music that was serious and sophisticated as well as country airs, comic songs, an appealing love duet, and elaborate coloratura arias. In addition, the songs abound in expressive animal imagery of birds, lambs, and wolves, to heighten the themes of freedom, innocence, and villainy.

After an elaborate Italian sinfonia overture, the first comic air is Cupid's "Oh, Why Will You Call Me Again," sung in answer to Urganda's request to captivate the heart of her beloved, Cymon. As the stage changes to a "magnificent garden," into which Cupid and the Loves descend, Cupid sings, to great comic effect, "The powers of a God/ Cannot quicken this clod,/ Alas! It is labor in vain." Another comic song is Dorcas's lament on the falseness of modern men, with her insistent question, "What can a Woman do?" with the same note of F repeated six times in the question. The ditty ends: "Since men are truly so unruly/ I tremble at Seventy two,/ I tremble, I tremble at seventy two."

In addition to injecting comedy, music is also used to identify characters, as in the case of the country lad, Linco, who is introduced singing "Care flies from the lad who is merry," and is soon entertaining the shepherdess with the lively country air set in 6/8 time, "I Laugh and Sing." Linco's later air, sung to comfort Sylvia at the end of the third act and written to be rendered allegro, "Sing High Derry Derry,"maintains the same character.

The integration of music into the plot line of the play is gracefully accomplished. When Cymon first discovers Sylvia sleeping on the riverbank, the music voices his falling in love. During the singing of his air, "All amaze!/ Wonder, praise,/ Here forever could I gaze!", Cymon advances toward the sleeping figure, then retires fearfully, then advances more boldly, only to retire again, both the melody and the tempo expressing his changing emotions. Similarly, in the fifth act, Cymon enters "in confusion and out of breath," in search of Sylvia. His air, marked *Allegro con Spirito,* "Torn from Me, Torn from Me," is preceded by a lengthy, three-part composition, the sinfonia, during which he runs off and returns several times, his actions dramatizing the racked emotions expressed by the rapid treble notes.

The most popular song of the play was that sung by Sylvia as she is being ordered to the black tower by Urganda, "Though various deaths surround me,/ No terrors can confound me" (5.1.99–100). Its graceful melody is finely ornamented and it contains impressive coloratura passages, especially in the rendition of the word "glory" in the line "I glory in my love!" and in the word "smile" in the last line of the song, "To Smile on Guilty Power."

Since the vocal pyrotechnics of coloratura passages were sure to please an eighteenth-century audience, Arne had wisely included them in Urganda's air, "Hence Every Hope and Every Fear!" which incorporates all the features of the rage aria of Italian opera, with the word "vengeance" receiving the most elaborate vocal treatment. Even the first Demon of Revenge, played by the celebrated bass singer, Champness, was given coloratura moments, ominously descending stepwise for seven tones on the word "torments."

The extraordinary success of the music in communicating the mood, characterizations, and dramatic movement of the play, in addition to the expert use of transformations to create a wonderland setting, and the care taken by Garrick in getting up "new scenes, dresses, machinery and other decorations"[15] combined to make *Cymon* a triumph of showmanship. Garrick presented the play sixty-four times during the next seven seasons, a remarkable record for a Christmas play in a repertory theater. *Cymon* continued to be staged throughout the century. By 1791 the spectacle had been heightened to include "a Grand Procession of the Hundred Knights of Chivalry, and the Representation of an Ancient Tournament," and some new music had been written by Stephen Storace and Thomas Shaw.[16] In 1850, nearly a century later, Garrick's still-popular *Cymon* was adapted by James Robinson Planché for production at the Lyceum Theatre where it became a nineteenth-century favorite.

*Christmas Tale* (1773).   Garrick's fluffy 1773 holiday offering, *A Christmas Tale,* was an immediate success, containing a satisfying blending of pleasing music, stunning set decoration, and general and inoffensive moral propositions. Another seraglio play, *A Christmas Tale* is set in a beautiful faraway land where magic abounds and where young men are expected to perform "some uncommon act of valor" in order to establish their manhood. After some slight deviations from the path of virtue, Floridor, the son of the "Good Magician" Bonoro, is united with the lady of his affections, Camilla, with the blessings of his benign father and to the acclamation of a Grand Chorus, largely because he has been true to the code of "Valor, Constancy and Honor." The play was an immediate success for Garrick and for his set designer, Phillipe Jacques De Loutherbourg, demonstrating once again Garrick's sensitive insight into the rapidly developing tastes of his audience for scenic design.

The benevolent father motif which permeates the spirit of the play is sounded in the Prologue by Father Christmas who, accompanied by cooks, scullions, and pastry-cooks, invites the audience, "my children," to a traditional English Christmas feast, promising them that, if they behave and if they bring good stomachs and swallow everything, they will enjoy it thoroughly. He urges them to give themselves up to the delightful and unreflective land of magic, suggesting:

> Clear well your minds from politics and spleen,
> Hear my Tale out—see all that's to be seen!

Even the customary mocking references to fops, fair ladies, and critics which usually appear in Garrick's Prologues have been softened in this, a prelude to the land of enchantment.

The good magician, Bonoro, troubled by his son's general lack of seriousness and his dalliance with the virtuous Camilla, enjoins him to destroy his rival, Nigromant, the leader of the evil spirits who formerly molested the world, but are now imprisoned by Bonoro in his castle. Bonoro gives his son his wand for protection and promises to render the proper incantations, but he cautions Floridor that these are only aids which the young man himself must activate: "Valor, Constancy and Honor must render all my charms effectual."

Although he is of good heart and right intentions, Floridor fails his first test, to guard the evil spirits while Bonoro absents himself to deliver the requisite incantations. Floridor assigns the task of watchman to Tycho so that he may have one more visit with his beloved Camilla, but Tycho is lulled to sleep by the seductive spirits, and the evil spirits make their escape. Though agitated by his son's misbehavior, the kindly Bonoro is nevertheless disarmed by Floridor's sincerity and sends him off with his blessing to restore order, joining in a melodious trio with the lovers.

Tycho, newly appointed squire to Floridor by Bonoro, is once again duped by a female spirit and loses Floridor's sword and shield, making the young knight's quest almost hopeless until he meets the old hag, Grinnelda, who is Camilla in disguise. In his desperation Floridor swears obedience to the crone, in return for the recovery of his sword and shield. Although Floridor refuses to part with a chaplet given him by Camilla as a love token, Grinnelda restores his sword and shield to him. The young man approaches the castle of Nigromant, strong of heart, and plunges into the fiery lake to do battle with the evil magician.

Floridor's moment of triumph in vanquishing Nigromant and leading the Evil Spirit and his retinue out in chains is momentarily interrupted by the discovery of his beloved Camilla and her woman, Robinette, as prisoners in the seraglio. And the joy of the lovers' reunion is further interrupted by the arrival of a message from Grinnelda demanding the fulfillment of his vow of obedience. When the young prince destroys the letter to appease Camilla, the stage directions note: "It thunders and grows dark. Flames of fire are seen through the seraglio windows. All but Floridor quit the place, shrieking." But Floridor retains the fortitude that is born of a clear conscience. When Grinnelda appears and demands his love, he reluctantly agrees, but he cannot be happy. "Draw me, tear me to pieces with wild horses, my last breath shall sigh Camilla. For I am her's and her's alone" (5.1.189–90). The stage directions indicate: "The stage grows light, and Camilla quitting at once the form of the old woman, assumes her real character and dress." As the reunited lovers share their joy, Bonoro descends in a cloud and blesses the union, to the sung acclamation of all the characters.

The constancy of the love of Floridor and Camilla is heightened by being conrasted with the uncertainty of the romance of Robinette, Camilla's saucy waiting lady, and Tycho, Floridor's squire. Robinette is the perfect soubrette, dictating behavior to each of her suitors, the good-hearted Tycho, who is melancholy over his immediate success in love, and the elderly Faladel, who is innately foolish. She insists that each adopt the opposite pose, Tycho to assume mirth, Faladel to act with gravity; thus she perceives one as her monkey and the other as her owl. Most of the comedy of the piece occurs in the fast-paced dialogue of these characters. The suitors offer love poetry of equal inferiority to their lady, as may be judged by one stanza of Faladel's "ode":

> Alack-a-day!
> You would not stay.
> I followed gay,
> Like faithful Tray
> With you to play,
> Or here to stay,
> At feet to lay.
> (3.2.61–7)

This is on a par with Tycho's song:

> Sweet Robinette,
> Your eyes are jet,
> And teeth are lily white
> Your cheeks are roses,
> Lips are posies
> And your nose is
> Wond'rous bright.
> (3.2.163–75)

In addition, there is an amusing satire on the town as Tycho interviews each of the evil spirits who have been imprisoned years earlier by Bonoro because they were "molesting society." The evil spirits reveal themselves as a Jesuit, an attorney, a poetical spirit, a political spirit who had been a statesman, a gamester, an actress, a glutton, and a woman of quality. The catalogue of devils is reminiscent of Garrick's early *Lethe* in both its members and its mood of gentle satire. In a moment of self-mockery that had become characteristic of his plays, the author has Tycho ask the actress: "What, have you singers and musicians among you?" She replies emphatically: "O yes, and dancers, actors, authors and managers too" (2.1.231–32).

Although the music for *The Christmas Tale,* composed by Charles Dibdin, was not inspired, it was successful in filling a functional role and advancing the plot line, as it heightened the mood. Dibdin composed a lavish score of thirty-two pieces in which the songs, at key moments of the play, substitute for verbal dialogue, rather than simply embellish it. For instance, Camilla awards a wreath as a love token to Floridor as he prepares to ride off to demonstrate valor, constancy, and honor in the song, "O take this wreath." In a tender trio in which he is joined by Floridor and Camilla, Bonoro later gives his blessing to his son as he leaves to conquer Nigromant and capture the evil spirits. Floridor's song, "Cruel fiends pursue me," at the beginning of Part IV has both an expository and dramatic function as the young prince relates his mishaps and summons his strongest resolution. As the tension mounts, two songs assume central importance in the play: when Floridor meets Nigromant, each challenges the other in the ringing song, "Stripling traitor"; later, when the whole palace bursts into flames upon Floridor's destroying the message of Grinnelda, Floridor martials his courage in the stirring, "Let the loud thunder rattle."

Garrick had succeeded in writing a play in which music functioned as a truly equal partner with the dramatic text; in addition to its usual functions on stage of providing emphasis, heightening atmosphere, and contributing melodic decoration to the play, the music in *The Christmas Tale* also established characterization, provided dialogue, and advanced the dramatic line.

The spectacular scenic design of *The Christmas Tale* enhanced the music and text and delighted playgoers. It was the work of Phillipe Jacques De Loutherbourg, a remarkable Alsatian painter newly arrived in London from the Continent and contracted by Garrick for the 1772–73 season. For this, his first assignment, he painted eight scenes, four of them highly detailed rural scenes, such as had won him acclaim in Paris. They include a beautiful landscape; a magnificent garden, luxurious with flowers; a dark and ominous wood, which opens upon the castle and fiery lake, home of Nigromant, the evil magician; and a sunrise view of the sea and a castle in the distance. De Loutherbourg's interior scenes were equally detailed: Bonoro's

cell, surrounded by prisons for the evil spirits; and a Grand Apartment in the Seraglio. The special effects that the scene designer arranged enchanted the audience: as Floridor visits Camilla while the
evil spirits whom he was left to guard escape, the stage directions
note that "the objects in the garden vary their colors." The audience
was startled by the varicolored lights. One spectator described it
thus: "It was a sudden transition in a forest scene, where the foliage
varies from green to blood colour. This contrivance was entirely new;
and the effect was produced by placing different coloured silks in the
flies, or side scenes, which turned on a pivot, and with lights behind,
which so illumined the stage, as to give the effect of enchantment."[17]

Other moments of spectacular excitement occurred when the prison
gates burst open, allowing the escape of the evil spirits, who "enter
promiscuously and riotously express their joy." Later, in a scene designated only a "a prospect of rocks," the rocks burst asunder to reveal
the castle and fiery lake of Nigromant. When Floridor later disregards the message of Grinnelda, the seraglio palace bursts into
flames, which gradually devour the castle. The flames and ruins of
the castle vanish to reveal a moonlit scene. De Loutherbourg had improved upon the use of transparencies that had been in use at Drury
Lane since *Harlequin's Invasion* in 1759 and he was able to use the
advanced lighting system which Garrick had introduced in 1765, following his trip to Paris. Even critics who berated the play for its lack
of seriousness found themselves charmed by the scenic design. Horace
Walpole called the designs "the most beautiful scenes next to those
in the opera at Paradise."[18]

Successfully integrating a simple and incredible tale with pleasing,
functional music and elaborate and spectacular scenic design, *A
Christmas Tale* established itself as an immediate success, bringing
very substantial returns to the playwright and his collaborating
artists.

## Later Operatic Works

***A Peep Behind the Curtain*** (1767).   The success of *A Peep Behind the Curtain; or, the New Rehearsal* was a tribute to the eclectic
genius of David Garrick, as well as an acknowledgment of his practical acumen in managing Drury Lane. The play is a successful amal-
gam of drama, set in the rehearsal tradition, and music, played to the
contemporary taste, both of these dashed with pungent satire.

Garrick's choice of subtitle, "The New Rehearsal," placed his work within the English tradition of using rehearsal plays for satiric purposes. *A Peep Behind the Curtain* depicts a morning in the life of a pompous playwright, Glib, who is witnessing the rehearsal of one act of his newly written musical play, "Orpheus." Garrick cleverly accomplished the wedding of theatrical burlesque and serious music by identifying Glib's play as a burletta. Thus the second act of *A Peep Behind the Curtain* is the supposed rehearsal of an English burletta on the theme of Orpheus's journey to the underworld to rescue his wife, Eurydice, with serious burletta music from an original score by François Barthelemon.

Because of great "solicitations" made to Patent, the theatre manager, he has agreed to rehearse one act of Glib's burletta "with dress and decorations as if it were really before an audience." Glib, who possesses all the characteristics of Buckingham's Bayes, has thereupon invited guests, Sir Toby Fuz and Lady Fuz, with their ingenuous daughter, Fanny Fuz, to attend the rehearsal. During the performance Miss Fuz runs off with her lover, Wilson, according to their carefully engineered plan. Her mother's discovery of this fact causes the entire party to leave and brings all action to a halt, as the chagrined author promises the manager delivery of the second act of the burletta during the following week.

Glib's supposed creation, the burletta "Orpheus," is an amusing musical treatment of the Orpheus legend which depicts a harried Orpheus whose sleep is interrupted by Eurydice who "thumps and scratches," beggging him for delivery from Hades. Before he makes his awesome journey, however, he attempts to placate his mistress, the fiery Rhodope. When this attempt fails, he puts her to sleep with his magical lyre, which he takes with him to charm the irascible old shepherd he meets in the countryside on his way to the underworld. Soon, the old man, a chorus of shepherds, and the sheep, cows, and goats are dancing to the music of Orpheus's strings, and are led offstage by Orpheus in a grand chorus of singing and dancing. Glib exults: "Every beast upon his hind legs!" His only regret is: "I did intend that houses and trees (according to the old story) should have joined in the dance, but it would have crowded the stage too much."

The comedy of the burletta "Orpheus" results largely from the juxtaposition of farcical actions onstage and serious music from the orchestra. The burletta, a short musical play built upon the elaboration of a single jest or humorous incident communicated musically and visually, had been a popular type on the English stage for almost twenty years. Introduced by traveling Italian companies in 1748 and later adapted as an English form by Kane O'Hara in *Midas* (1764), the burletta always employed serious, technically sophisticated music drawn from a variety of musical styles and types.[19]

Barthelemon's score, a very creditable specimen of burletta music, opens with an Italian sinfonia, and includes a patter song in the ballad opera style, a vengeance aria and *recitativo secco* from Italian opera seria, a ballet such as was included in every serious Italian opera, a melodious love song, and a folk song, before ending in a rousing vaudeville. The use of diversified musical styles is a key factor in the satire: "The musical thrust of the burletta, then is achieved by the juxtaposition of serious musical genres and the expectation they arouse and comic words that deflate such expectancies. At times the music is absolutely serious when taken without its text. At other times, however, certain mannerisms of the genre are deliberately exaggerated."[20] The influential *Theatrical Observer* of October 23, 1767 made the qualitative judgment that the music was "masterly to an uncommon degree," echoing the general enthusiasm of the playhouse audiences.

Another factor in the play's success was the newly attained public affection bestowed on actors and actresses, largely through the celebrity status given the profession by Garrick himself. Garrick exploited the warmth of public feeling, and his play contains good-natured amusing sallies against the popular veteran actor, Thomas King, against the effervescent Kitty Clive, and against Garrick himself. The play is peopled with a number of recognizable lesser characters from the world of Drury Lane: Saunders, the carpenter; Hopkins, the prompter; Johnson, the housekeeper; and the women sweepers, all of whom simulate the activities of the theater during the early morning hours.

*A Peep Behind the Curtain* remained popular throughout the Garrick era, a tribute to the playwright's increasing ability to utilize serious music functionally, rather than decoratively, to attain dramatic ends and to his characteristic geniality in furthering camaraderie between audience and players.

*May Day; or, The Little Gypsy* (1775). *May Day*, Garrick's last musical play, is a slight one-act piece which, nonetheless, attained considerable distinction due to its characterizations of good-natured country folk, its ebullience of good spirits, and its delightful music, written by the distinguished theatrical composer, Dr. Thomas Augustine Arne. In the "Advertisement" which preceded the printed edition of the play Garrick claimed that the piece was written simply as a vehicle for Harriet Abrams, a seventeen-year-old singer who was making her debut in the role of the Little Gypsy. The play was well received by the audience and there was great enthusiasm for its music.

*May Day* is peopled with the simple country types that Garrick seemed to create almost without effort and its comedy is broadly farcical. Furrow, a sixty-five-year-old wealthy farmer who has sent his son Will to London to forget the romance that the father has thwarted, proceeds to fall in love with the high-spirited Fanny Belton, the Little Gypsy, unaware that she is his son's former fiancée in disguise. The plot is further complicated by the fact that the late Squire Goodwill has left a legacy of £100 to the first couple married annually on May Day. Thus, not only do father and son vie for the same prize, but they wish to acquire it with the same bride. Dozey, the tippling town clerk; Clod, Furrow's outspoken servant; Dolly, Will Furrow's spirited and mischievous sister, and the bevy of country lasses, all watch the love affairs with great interest.

According to old Furrow's plan, Fanny, a fine mimic, is to disguise herself as the Little Gypsy and come to the maypole on the village green to tell the fortunes of the country lads and lasses. Dolly, Furrow's daughter, a young lady of equal vivacity, is to play the role of the Little Gypsy's mother. The country folk are duped, and Will and the Gypsy take advantage of the situation to reaffirm their love in an exalted air, "Passions of the purest nature," before the appearance of Old Furrow, who has come to claim both bride and legacy. But the cunning Fanny persuades the elder Furrow that she could not be truly happy if the father did not first satisfy the son. When Furrow agrees to listen to Will, the son claims the Little Gypsy for his own. Though perplexed, the old farmer finds himself unable to retract his promise to Fanny. The villagers urge a reconciliation, and the play ends with a spirited finale, with Clod, Will, the Gypsy, Furrow, and the villagers all joining in, evidence of peace restored:

> When the heart is unkind,
> With the frost of the mind,
> Benevolence melts it like May.
> (2.521–23)

As a musical theater piece, *May Day* is interesting in its demonstration of the effect of selected serious music on an essentially nonmusical comedy. In contrast to Dibdin's fulsome score for *The Christmas Tale,* Arne's music for *May Day* consists of an overture and only ten airs, plus a finale. Only five of the airs are dramatic, making a contribution to the advancement of the plot, whereas the other five fulfill the lesser conventional functions of theatrical music: communicating mood, heightening characterization, or extending dialogue. All pleased the audience with their lightness and melody.

Those songs that may be described as dramatic occur at key moments in the play. The first of these is the amusing "What's a poor simple clown/ to do in the town," a song highly reminiscent of that of Linco in *Linco's Travels.* The dramatic nature of the song is stressed when Clod, in response to questions on his recent adventures in London, replies: ". . . my song that I got there will tell you better all about it than I can" (2.37–38). His subsequent sung description of Londoners allows for gentle satire on both the ladies of fashion and the fops about town. The song, placed early in the play, serves to emphasize the fact that Will Furrow, in contrast to the foolish fops, is sober and lovelorn. Another successful dramatic use of serious music is Dolly's spirited air "Young maids and young swains," which uses the ballad form of verse and refrain. This song serves to divert the attention of the villagers and thus allow Will and Fanny a few moments of cherished privacy.

Even those songs that have no dramatic function are light and pretty, contributing to the ambience of the play. "O lovely sweet May!" sung by the village lads and lasses when they have finished dancing around the maypole, has an infectious gaiety which establishes the mood of the play. The first two songs rendered by the Little Gypsy, "Hail, Spring!" and the more elaborate "Spread thy rich mantle, sweet May," are delicate, charming melodies, confirming the villagers' conception of the young girl as "a perfect nightingale."

Moreover, Arne's compositions were technically sophisticated. The overture, interesting in its early sonata form, was scored for flutes, oboes, and strings. The songs themselves contain unusual orchestral coloring, such as the pronounced use of woodwinds to imitate the voice in "Spread thy green mantle"; and the use of two bassoons echoing the male voice in the love duet, "Passions of the purest nature."[21]

The critics were enthusiastic, *Town and Country Magazine* (November, 1775) noting that the music "has considerable merit, and it is well adapted to the airs." In addition, the reviewer for *The Westminster Magazine* (November, 1775) wrote: "The music of the Overture and the Finale were remarkably light and pretty: some of the Airs also did Dr. Arne credit." The collaboration between a distinguished London theatrical composer and an important London playwright had been successful. Garrick, now close to retirement, once again had contributed work of a very high caliber to English musical theater.

## Garrick's Topical Musical Plays

Garrick had become so adept at writing within the context of a musical theater that, toward the end of his career, not only major works but lesser ones as well were designed to be coupled with music. Two short musical works are especially noteworthy since each was written to exploit the fame and newsworthiness of a particular contemporary event. Each brought a glamorous public incident, tailored to the demands of theatrical presentation, to the London stage; and each was commercially successful, demonstrating once again the accuracy of Garrick's view of the taste of his audience. Garrick's two short topical musical plays were *The Jubilee* (1769) and *The Institution of the Garter* (1771).

*The Jubilee* (1769). *The Jubilee,* Garrick's applause-winning 1769 afterpiece, derives from the failure of the much-heralded Shakespeare Jubilee in Stratford in September, 1769, which left the playwright with a debt of £2000.[22]

Garrick's notion of recovering part of the debt seems to have crystallized upon his hearing that his friend and professional rival, George Colman, planned a comedy, entitled *Man and Wife; or, The Shakespeare Jubilee,* based on the same event. Garrick recalled with characteristic candor, in a letter to the Reverend Evan Lloyd on December 4, 1769, the exact circumstances of his play's composition. He writes that, upon hearing of Colman's plan,

I set myself down to work, & in a day & a half produc'd our Jubilee— which has had more success than any thing I Ever remember. . . I have really given Such a true picture, I mean for resemblance of our Stratford Business, that You are in y$^e$ midst of it at Drury Lane playhouse—I wrote y$^e$ petite piece upon one Single Idea, which struck me at y$^e$ time, & Which has fortunately struck y$^e$ audience in y$^e$ Same Manner—it is this—I suppose

an Irishman (excellently perform'd by Moody) to come from Dublin to See
yᵉ Pageant—he is oblig'd to lye in a post Chaise all Night—undergoes all
kind of fatigue & inconvenience to see yᵉ Pageant, but unluckily goes to
Sleep as yᵉ Pageant passes by; & returns to Ireland without knowing any
thing of yᵉ Matter.[23]

The result was a two-part afterpiece entitled *The Jubilee* which Garrick brought out on October 14, 1769, less than six weeks after the
disastrous Stratford Jubilee. The audience responded enthusiastically
and the play attained eighty-eight performances during the first season, a record number during any one season for an afterpiece during
the whole century.

Having established the stock Irishman as the center of his comedy,
Garrick injected a note of topical humor by having his own popular
performers, Joseph Vernon and Charles Bannister, shown in a moment of gleeful inebriation. This technique of good-naturedly satirizing his own performers who commanded the affections of the
audience had been highly successful in *A Peep*, just two years earlier.

The play consists of six scenes, four of them of farcical comedy en-
livened with good music, and two of them serious tributes to Shakespeare, almost reverential in tone, remnants of the Stratford Jubilee.
Each of the serious scenes occurs at the end of the act, assuring its
maximum impact.

The first scene introduces the townsfolk of Stratford who are both
confused and frightened by the clamor caused by the Jubilee and who
believe that, at bottom, " 'Tis certainly a plot of the Jews and Pap-
ishes." When one of the old women inquires about the steward of the
Jubilee, "the ring leader of the Jubillo," a position Garrick had held
in the actual Stratford Jubilee, Ralph replies in a line written with
Garrick's characteristic self-mocking comedy: "Yes, I ha' seen him.
Not much to be seen, though, . . . He's not so big as I, but a great
deal plumper."

Into the carnival-like atmosphere of the second scene enters the
crotchety Irishman, irritated by the discomforts of an evening spent
in a post chaise. When he inquires of a musician about the nature of
the Jubilee, the latter answers in a sprightly air that is filled with the
self-mockery that is the hallmark of this little play:

> This is, Sir, a Jubilee
> Crowded without

> company,
> Riot without jollity,
> That's a Jubilee
> ................
> Odes, Sir without poetry
> Music without melody
> Singing without
> harmony.
>
> (1.2.37–51)

Garrick here paraphrases and thus reduces the effectiveness of a comic description of the Stratford Jubilee which his rival, Samuel Foote, had injected into his own farce, *The Devil Upon Two Sticks,* for the sake of topical comedy.

No doubt the funniest scene is that set in the White Lion Inn Yard in which people enter the crowded stage, some with bags, newly arrived at Stratford, some seeking food and drink, some in search of lodging, some simply trying to find old friends. Everyone and everything seems to work at cross-purposes, with the harried waiters, moving ever so swiftly, attempting to placate their unhappy patrons. The Irishman, watching, muses: "There's no pleasure at all like a Jubilee. The delight is to be wanting everything and get nothing, to see everybody busy and not know what they're about" (1.3.57–59). Bannister and Vernon, as themselves, enter, "Mr. Vernon with the Mulberry cup in his hand and fuddled." Nevertheless, they sing a delightful air on the mulberry tree, before drums, fifes, and bells ring, announcing the beginning of the pageant.

The pageant itself is a sumptuous procession of favorite characters from nineteen Shakespearean plays, each character depicted at a significant moment in the play. The procession is introduced by nine male dancers with tambourines, the three Graces, nine female dancers as the nine Muses, two standard-bearers, and two fifes and two drums. The comedies are separated from the tragedies and histories by the appearance of the Pageant Chorus, composed of six boys and twenty men costumed as Arcadian shepherds. They render Bickerstaff's air "Hence, ye profane!" and are followed by the three Graces, Apollo with his lyre, the statue of Shakespeare "supported by the Passions and surrounded by the Seven Muses with their trophies," a kettledrum drawn in a car, and six trumpets.

Garrick's well-known attention to detail is demonstrated in the

completeness of his directions for each Shakespearean play. The pageant of *The Tempest* is to appear thus:"

> *Tempest*
> Sailor with a banner
> Ariel with a wand, raising a tempest
> A ship in distress sailing down the stage—
> Prospero with a wand
> Miranda
> Caliban with a wooden bottle and
>     2 sailors all drunk

The result was a scene of visual delight, whose richness and vastness,
and whose mechanical daring in moving the ship downstage, catered
to the growing love of spectacle.

Garrick was thus able to stage the elaborate procession of Shakespearean characters that had been designed for the Stratford festival
but had been sacrificed to the torrential rains of September.

The scene shifts quickly to the Stratford street for the second part
of the play, which unites the visiting Irishman and the townspeople.
Two young girls appear, one of whom swears, "I dote upon Shake-
spur," while the other sings skeptically about the subject of the festival. The Irishman, attracted by the "Jubilee wenches," is about to
pursue them when he learns that the pageant has already taken place
while he was sleeping in the inn-yard. Chagrined, he considers, "And
now I must return back in the rain, as great a fool as those who hate
to stay in their own country and return from their travels as much
improved as myself shall when I go back to Kilkenny" (2.2.20–24),
a mild attack on one of Garrick's favorite satirical targets, the young
men about town who insisted on making the Grand Tour.

The final scene "is a magnificent transparent one in which the capital characters of Shakespeare are exhibited at full length, with Shakespeare's statue in the middle crowned by Tragedy and Comedy, fairies
and cupids surrounding him, and all the banners waving at the upper
end. Then enter the Dancers, and then the Tragic and Comic Troops,
and range themselves in the scene." After a dance of the graces and
muses, the chief Shakespearean characters come forward individually,
each singing solo a verse of a roundelay, before going back to join the
chorus.

Garrick's audience responded to this clever little exercise in thea-
trics. *The Jubilee* was a feast for the eyes and was pleasing to the ears;

it included Garrick's country types who, by this time, had become favorites with the audience; and it contained one truly great comic scene, set in the yard of the White Lion Inn. Besides pleasing his audience, Garrick must have pleased himself: he was able to salvage both the elaborate procession of Shakespearean characters and most of the music that had been prepared for his unfortunate Stratford festival.

*The Institution of the Garter* (1771).   Garrick made a second successful use of the playcrafting techniques he had capitalized on two years earlier in *The Jubilee* with *The Institution of the Garter*. He again seized upon an event of widespread interest, this time George III's magnanimous installation of nine princes and nobles as Knights of the Order of the Garter in July, 1771, at Windsor Castle.

Garrick had two reasons for incorporating this event into the Drury Lane repertory: public interest was running high because of the extraordinarily large number of those being honored, and, more pragmatically, the current Lord Chamberlain, Granville Leveson-Gower, the second Earl Gower, was one of those elevated. Gower was important as the official to whom copies of all plays had to be submitted for approval prior to production, and Garrick decided to fashion a piece to honor him, making use of the kind of materials he had used previously: low characters in farcical scenes, pleasing music, and a sumptuous procession to be executed in a reverential atmosphere. As the framework for this theatrical piece, Garrick used a serious dramatic poem by Gilbert West, "The Institution of the Garter" (1742).

The considerable popularity of *The Institution of the Garter* was due primarily to its topicality and to its ebullient good spirits. As a theater piece, it was less well integrated than *The Jubilee,* to which it had many similarities. Nevertheless, it was enthusiastically received at Drury Lane and performed thirty-three times that season.

## Shorter Musical Works

*Linco's Travels* (1767).   *Linco's Travels,* described by John O'Keefe as "a little piece of wit and sarcasm in rhyme and song," is a slight piece of some 170 lines written by Garrick to provide Thomas King, his stellar comedian who had recently endeared himself to theater audiences as Linco, the merry country lad in *Cymon,* with a vehicle for his benefit night on April 6, 1767. Linco is depicted returning from his travels abroad to Arcadia, where he is welcomed by a gathering of Arcadian men and women. Only Linco and Dorcas, the seventy-two-year-old countrywoman of *Cymon,* speak; in addition, Linco has two airs composed by Michael Arne, who had written the music for *Cymon.* These were, according to O'Keeffe, "very beautiful."[24] *Linco's Travels,* because it was so slender a work, was presented as an interlude, between the mainpiece and the afterpiece. Its significance lies not so much in its creditable record of performance as an interlude, but rather because the characterization of Linco had been so successful and had made so deep an impression on eighteenth-century audiences that Linco now took on an independent existence. Indeed, it was Garrick's dramatic character, Linco, as well as the actor, Thomas King, who was the object of the audience's affection.

   ***The Theatrical Candidates*** (1775).   Although a slight piece, *The Theatrical Candidates* is a testament to the continuing creative vitality of David Garrick, even in the final year of his professional life. Having arranged and overseen the lavish redecoration of Drury Lane Theatre that had been accomplished by the Adam brothers, he sought a way to mark the opening of the 1775–76 season in the sumptuous new surroundings.

   Filled with a sense of new beginnings, he wrote a musical piece in a form that was new to him, the musical prelude, engaging William Bates, a successful ballad-opera composer, to set the music. Perhaps it was this sense of newness that prompted Garrick to ask his audience for reevaluation and reaffirmation of the hierarchy of dramatic types to be played in the new Drury Lane.

   Mercury, god of wits and thieves, appears on stage to announce that two rival dames above have requested permission to leave Olympus to live forever in Drury Lane. Mercury leaves the audience to examine the rival claims, while he returns to Apollo for his wise judgment, with a pleasant satiric song:

> When the female tongues begin,
> Who has ears to beat the din,
>         And wings to fly, will stay?
>         I'll away, I'll away.

   Tragedy enters, to a march, followed by Comedy, each appealing in song for the support of the audience. Then the two enter into a verbal duel. Tragedy accuses Comedy of producing "stale sentiments" which had originated with Tragedy and of bringing forth "motley, dull sententious farces" which sickened the town. Comedy replies, attacking the bastardization of tragedy through the mixing of dramatic types:

> For all this mighty pother,
> Have you not laughed with one eye, cried with t'other?

Tragedy directs the essential question to the audience: "Which will you choose?"; Comedy qualifies: "Sour Her, or smiling Me?/ There are but two of us."

This is the cue for the entrance of Harlequin, who upbraids the ladies for their pretentiousness and lack of candor:

> For all your airs, sharp looks and sharper nails,
> Draggled you were till I held up your tails.

He then appeals to the audience:

> Deep thought and politics so stir your gall
> When you come here you should not think at all.

When Mercury enters, breathlessly bringing the wisdom of Apollo, all are content to receive his judgment. Apollo has decided that:

> You, Tragedy, must weep and love and rage,
> And keep your turn, but not engross the stage.

Comedy is instructed:

> And you, gay madam, gay to give delight,
> Must not, turned prude, encroach upon her right.

Tragedy and Comedy, then, are to share the stage at Drury Lane, each separately charming the audience, "Unless that Shakespeare bring you both together." Even Monsieur Harlequin may have his moments on stage, "whenever farce or song,/ Are sick and tired." Comedy, Tragedy, and Harlequin join Mercury in a rousing final chorus which asks the audience to confirm Apollo's judgment:

> 'Tis you must decree,
> For your praise is the key,
> To open the Temple of Fame.

In this, one of the last works he wrote for the stage, it was fitting that Garrick should bring once again to the audience at Drury Lane the question that had engaged his aspirations and consumed his energies for the whole of his career: how best to satisfy the playhouse audience while elevating their taste.[25] In *The Theatrical Candidates* he used music not simply to decorate the play, as he had done in his early career, nor even merely to advance the play, as he had done in his later years, but this time he had chosen music as the most effective framework in which to pose for his audience the essential questions about drama and its role in a civilized society.

## Chapter Four

# The Playwright and the God of His Idolatry: Adaptations of Shakespeare

The interdependence of actor and playwright that informed and shaped Garrick's writing of his comedic and musical works is central also to his selection of Shakespearean works to adapt to the stage of Drury Lane and to the effects he strove for in presenting them. His first concern in considering a play, either as actor or manager, was its actability. Did the chief roles lend themselves to direct and effective presentation? Were the scenes constructed so as to communicate conflict, passion, emotion? Did the action progress with sufficient speed to an effective climax? Further, Garrick considered whether or not a given play was likely to draw a strong audience response.

Garrick judged a number of significant Shakespearean plays to be effective vehicles because these questions could be answered positively concerning them. In addition to the operatic versions of *A Midsummer Night's Dream* and *The Tempest,* mentioned earlier, he fashioned ten Shakespearean plays for the stage of his day, attaining uncommon success with some, but meeting failure in one or two cases. In all his attempts, however, he professed a vital interest in attaining the authentic texts of Shakespeare's poetry and, for the most part, he made substantial progress in that direction. His devotion to Shakespeare spanned his whole career, his first adaptation, *Macbeth,* appearing in 1744 and his last, *Hamlet,* in 1772, almost thirty years later.

When Garrick arrived in London in 1737, he found only eleven of Shakespeare's plays in the repertory, most of them extravagant adaptations that were considerably different from the originals. Seeking a release from the weight of the bland verbiage of the Restoration and eighteenth-century adapters of Shakespeare, Garrick announced himself a true student of Shakespeare:

> 'Tis my chief wish, my joy, my only plan
> To lose no drop of that immortal man.

He addressed himself to the restoration, within the parameters acceptable to his audience, of the language, the poetry, the wit, the vivacity, and the complexity of England's foremost playwright.

## Macbeth (1744)

Garrick, riding the crest of his popularity as the town's newest and most exciting Shakespearean actor, was given the opportunity to present his own version of *Macbeth* on January 7, 1744. He promised to present the play "as Shakespeare wrote it." Although *Macbeth* was a favorite play on the London stage in the first half of the eighteenth century and had been presented over two hundred times since 1700, the play that Londoners witnessed was not Shakespeare's original work, but rather William Davenant's spectacular adaptation of it, rendered in 1694, a work significantly different from Shakespeare's in conception, characterization, and execution.

**Davenant's *Macbeth*.** In reworking *Macbeth* for his Restoration audience, Davenant had two strong objectives: to achieve symmetry and clarity and to present the play in operatic style.

Symmetry was attained by balancing characters, a practice which is "a natural consequence of the systematic creation of typical rather than complex characters."[1] Thus, Lady Macduff in her goodness and wifeliness is elevated to become a foil to Lady Macbeth; and the witches meet Macduff and his wife on the heath at the end of act 2 to give them a triple prophecy parallel to that given Macbeth. Clarity was attained through a general simplification of the plot and through a reduction of the language of Shakespeare's poetry to language that is literal and banal. The operatic stye of Davenant's *Macbeth* was superimposed on the play chiefly through the addition of selected music and the use of stage machinery to achieve spectacular effects.

**Garrick's *Macbeth*.** To devise an authentic Shakespearean text, Garrick sought direction from the most recent scholarly edition, that of Lewis Theobald, in addition to corresponding with prominent Shakespearean scholars, including Samuel Johnson and William Warburton. Occasionally, he emended the text himself, in deference to the exigencies of effective eighteenth-century stage presentation; in about a dozen instances, he found it practical to retain the readings of Davenant, accepting the long-established tastes of his audience. In all, Garrick's text of *Macbeth,* which became the accepted acting version throughout the century, returned to the basic conception of Shakespeare, retained most of the original poetry, and emerged as "the most accurate stage version of a Shakespearean play which had appeared since 1671."[2]

As he altered the text, Garrick made three kinds of changes: substitutions, deletions, and additions. The substitutions were usually of vocabulary, as Garrick bowed to the eighteenth-century demand for refined and genteel language. He often substitutes "heaven" for "God." "In the great hand of God I stand" is altered to "In the great hand of heav'n I stand" (2.1.247); and Malcolm's "Good God betimes remove/ The means" becomes "Good Heav'n betimes remove/ The means" (4.3.92). Macbeth's plea to the Doctor to "Cleanse the stuff'd bosom of the perilous stuff" becomes, in Garrick's version, "Cleanse the full bosom of that perilous stuff" (5.3.46).

When Garrick deleted material, he did so to focus the attention of the audience upon the major characters. For instance, Garrick took Lady Macbeth offstage immediately after the discovery of Duncan's body, since she distracted attention from the main stage business. Garrick also deleted lines that he considered unnecessary to the dramatic development of the play, so as to quicken the pace of dramatic action. To this end, he pruned the concluding lines to the dagger soliloquy and reduced the scene in which Macbeth negotiates with Banquo's murderers.

Garrick believed in the importance of strong and effective conclusions to individual scenes. Thus, he made two significant omissions in the play: first, he excised the Old Man's lines in 3.1: "God's benison go with you, and with those/ That would make good of bad, and friends of foes" so that the scene ends instead with Macduff's

> Well, may you see things well done there. Adieu!
> Lest our old robes fit easier than our new!
>
> (3.1.48—49)

A second instance occurs in the powerful fifth act as Macbeth takes leave of Lady Macbeth, leaving her in the care of the doctor. Shakespeare's scene ends with the doctor's tag line:

> Were I from Dunsinane away and clear,
> Profit again should hardly draw me here.

Garrick excises this so that the scene ends with Macbeth's ominous lines:

> Bring it after me!
> I will not be afraid of death and bane
> Till Birnam Forest come to Dunsinane.
>                                   (5.3.62–64)

Such changes were subtle, contributing to the overall economy and effectiveness of the stage presentation.

On the other hand, the additions Garrick made were spectacular and won the raves of the audience. He significantly enlarged the witches' scene in 3.6, cutting three lines at the end of the original scene and adding an extended musical scene for the witches, including "a Symphony, while Hecate places herself in the machine." Thus, he preserved some of the spectacular appeal of the Davenant adaptation. Undoubtedly, the most significant additions are made to 5.6, the scene in which Macbeth dies on stage. Garrick preserves the six lines of Macduff as he and Macbeth fight:

> This for my royal master Duncan!
> This for my bosom friend, my wife! and this for
> The pledges of her love and mine, my children!
>                   *Macbeth falls.*
> Sure there are remains to conquer.—I'll
> As a trophy bear away his sword to
> Witness my revenge.
>                   *Exit Macduff.*

Garrick then wrote an eight-line speech for Macbeth, as he lies alone dying on the ground:

> 'Tis done! the scene of life will quickly close.
> Ambition's vain, delusive dreams are fled,
> And now I wake to darkness, guilt and horror.
> I cannot bear it! Let me shake it off.—
> 'Twa'not be; my soul is clogged with blood.
> I cannot rise! I dare not ask for mercy.
> It is too late, hell drags me down, I sink,
> I sink—Oh!—my soul is lost forever!
> Oh! (Dies)
>                                   (5.6.73–81)

Although this passage violated Garrick's intent to present *Macbeth* as written by Shakespeare, and although the poetry is impoverished, if contrasted with the Shakespearean line, the speech was an acting tour de force for Garrick and was roundly applauded. Jean Georges Noverre, a French ballet master, has written graphically of the effectiveness of Garrick's rendition of this scene:

. . . the approach of death showed each instant on his face; his eyes became dim, his voice could not support the efforts he made to speak his thoughts. His gestures, without losing their expression, revealed the approach of the last moment; his legs gave way under him, his face lengthened, his pale and livid features bore the signs of suffering and repentance. At last, he fell; at that moment his crimes peopled his thoughts with the most horrible forms; terrified at the hideous picture which his past acts revealed to him, he struggled against death; nature seemed to make one supreme effort. His plight made the audience shudder, he clawed the ground and seemed to be digging his own grave, but the dread moment was nigh, one saw death in reality, everything expressed that instant which makes all equal. In the end he expires. The death rattle and the convulsive movements of the features, arms and breasts, gave the final touch to this terrible picture."[3]

Both of these significant additions made by Garrick were intentional deviations from the Shakespearean text in order to appeal to the sensibilities of an eighteenth-century audience which reveled in the excitement of both the spectacle and great acting. Garrick realized that his restoration of Shakespeare would have to be accomplished within parameters set by the taste of his audience.

In short, Garrick's *Macbeth* was not only a demonstration of the fact that exalted poetry could make a powerful impact when rendered on stage, but also of the happy proposition that the taste of a theater audience could be elevated in the overall, as long as its particular biases were honored. Garrick's adaptation of the play remained an audience favorite.

## *Romeo and Juliet* (1748)

In presenting *Romeo and Juliet* on November 19, 1748, during the first year of his managerial tenure, Garrick brought the play to Drury Lane for the first time in its history. In fact, Shakespeare's tale of the star-crossed lovers had not been presented on the stage of a patent theater in London since 1680. Although Samuel Pepys records his attending the opening night of the play at Lincoln's Inn Fields on March 1, 1662, *Romeo and Juliet* soon had to share billing with an alteration by James Howard, which caught the public fancy since it concluded with the lovers alive. Restoration audiences apparently found no difficulty in seeing a tragical Romeo one night and a tragicomic lover the next.[4]

Both Romeos were driven off the boards in 1680 by Thomas Otway's ostensible classical tragedy, *The History and Fall of Caius Marius*, a thinly disguised dramatization of *Romeo and Juliet,* herein named Marius and Lavinia. A predecessor of *Venice Preserv'd,* it contains many of the same ingredients: political plots, uprisings of the rabble, and unprincipled demagoguery; yet it retains unmistakable plot motifs from *Romeo and Juliet*, including the feud, the secret wedding, the magical potion, and, finally, the drinking of poison by Marius at the tomb of Lavinia. Otway retains Howard's fashionable ending in having Lavinia awaken before Marius dies and she subsequently stabs herself with his sword. In short, Otway's alteration replaced Shakespeare's grand poetry with prosaic Restoration language; it complicated the plot with unnecessary action; and it omitted the ominous element of fate that hovers over the Shakespearean play.

Theophilus Cibber, a controversial actor, presented one more version of *Romeo and Juliet* at the Haymarket in 1744. His play was closer to Shakespeare than Otway's, and although it ran for only ten performances, it had the catalytic value of focusing public attention on one of Shakespeare's neglected masterpieces.

**Garrick's *Romeo and Juliet*.**    Garrick followed the practice he had established in altering *Macbeth*: he returned to a scholarly edition of the Shakespearean text; he made certain substitutions in vocabulary; he deleted material unnecessary to dramatic progress; and he made certain showy and spectacular additions. As with *Macbeth*, Garrick's alteration of *Romeo and Juliet* was an overwhelming success and held the boards well into the nineteenth century.

In the "Advertisement" preceding the play Garrick indicates his practice of ridding the play of "jingle" and "quibble," which had prevented successful revival in the past. "Jingle" was Garrick's word for Shakespeare's use of rhyme in certain moments in the play in place of blank verse; "quibble" referred to some of the wordplay: the puns and the clever trifling with language with which the play is peppered.

Garrick's most significant deletion was the removal of Rosaline, the lady for whom Romeo pines and about whom he is teased in the first act, since Garrick believed this love may have been construed as a blemish on Romeo's character.

The fifth act contains two important additions Garrick made to the play: a funeral dirge written by Garrick and set to music by William Boyce was inserted and a seventy-five line death scene for Romeo was added. A foreign visitor, Count Frederick Kielmansegge, who saw the play, described it graphically: "In the play an entire funeral is represented, with bells tolling, and a choir singing. Juliet, feigning death, lies on a state bed with a splendid canopy over her, . . . The scene represents the interior of a church. . . nothing of the kind could be presented more beautifully or naturally."[5] Although the scene contributed nothing to the dramatic action, it was a crowd-pleaser, Francis Gentleman noting that "nothing could be better devised than a funeral procession to render the play thoroughly popular."[6]

Garrick's second addition, the new tomb scene, thrilled the audience. Romeo enters the tomb, finds the inanimate Juliet, and drinks the poison just as she awakens; a death scene of some seventy-five lines follows. Francis Gentleman suggests that nature was brought to its "most critical feelings" at this moment and Romeo's "affectionate transports, forgetting what he has done, fills the audience with a most cordial sympathy of satisfaction, which is soon dashed in both, by the poison's operating."[7] In Arthur Murphy's view, "the catastrophe, as it now stands, is the most affecting in the whole compass of the drama."[8]

That Garrick's descendants shared the enthusiasm of his contemporaries is evident in the fact that Garrick's tomb scene was used as late as 1875 by Charles Wyndham and apparently was not abandoned until Henry Irving's production of *Romeo and Juliet* in 1882, some 134 years after its inception.

Garrick in his alteration of *Romeo and Juliet* had admirably satisfied the adapter's criteria: it was a splendid acting vehicle and it drew the enthusiastic response of his audience.

## King Lear (1756)

Garrick's adaptation of *King Lear* derives substantially from his intimate knowledge of the character through acting the part, demonstrating, once again, the interdependence of playwright and actor. Although his early success in the role, which dated from 1742, was due to his splendid rendition of Tate's text, Garrick was anxious to abandon that text in favor of presenting a more authentic Shakespearean play to his audience.

**Tate's *Lear*.** Tate's version of *King Lear*, which had held the boards since 1681, was written in conformity with neoclassical canons and thus sought order in plot, clarity in language, the balancing of characters, and the observance of the unities. It maintained its popularity well beyond the Restoration because it celebrated poetic justice, ended happily, and communicated a strongly ethical point of view, all elements guaranteed to produce pleasure for eighteenth-century audiences.

To accomplish his aims, Tate had shifted emphasis from the character of Lear, who is at the center of Shakespeare's play, to the political implications of his actions. In addition, he created a love interest between Edgar and Cordelia. Thus Lear was not seen in the agony of his isolation, but rather as part of a mix of unhappy events involving his family and kingdom, as well as himself.

Tate had created a theatrical success, but had done so at the expense of the plot, characterization, sentiments, and language of the Shakespearean masterpiece. Nevertheless, despite sporadic objections to Tate's *Lear*, it was not displaced from the English stage until 1838.[9]

**Garrick's *Lear*.** In playing Lear, which soon became his most famous role, Garrick made gradual alterations in Tate's text which cut much of Tate's play and restored substantial elements of Shakespeare. Despite a desire to present a fully authentic Shakespearean play, Garrick dared not offend the contemporary taste of the audience by a complete reversion to the authentic text. Garrick's was, according to George Winchester Stone, Jr., "the dilemma of an eighteenth-century mind caught between an ideal liking for Shakespeare and a canny understanding of box-office appeal."[10]

Garrick's central view of Lear is that he is one whose distresses "proceeded from good qualities carry'd to excess of folly," as he explained in a letter to Edward Tighe, and this is the view that informed and structured his adaptation.[11] Accordingly, Garrick sought opportunities to demonstrate this in the character of Lear. He employed his usual techniques of substitution and deletion which he had used in *Macbeth* and *Romeo and Juliet*, but decided to forego any additions, such as those he had made to the earlier plays.

Garrick restored the first scene of Shakespeare's play in which Kent and Gloucester discuss the division of the kingdom and Gloucester discusses with near-lightness Edmund's bastardy, prefiguring Lear's first appearance in which he, too, will misunderstand a child. Garrick restored the original Shakespearean language, preferring the power of the muscular verse of the original play to Tate's prosaic, though clear verse. Garrick looked to the third-act heath scene as one in which the pain of Lear's isolation could be effectively dramatized, and in it he substituted the full-bodied, hearty language of Shakespeare for the pallid language of Tate.

One of the results of Garrick's restoration of Shakespeare's language was a redirection of emphasis in characterization. In Edmund's soliloquy on bastards, which opens Tate's play, the correct but colorless question of Tate's Edmund:

> . . . why am I then
> Depriv'd of a son's right, because I came not
> In the dull road that custom has prescribed?
>
> (1.1.2–4)

is discarded in favor of the robust language of the Shakespearean original:

> . . . Wherefore should I
> Stand in the plague of custom, and permit
> The curiosity of Nations to deprive me
> For that I am some twelve or fourteen moonshines
> Lag of a brother?
>
> (1.3.2–6)

The restoration of the entire passage establishes Edmund as someone of keen intellectual acumen, rather than simply Tate's caricature of unmitigated villainy.

Garrick's most significant deletion was the excision of Tate's entire fourth-act scene of dalliance between Regan and Edmund, in which the stage directions indicate the two are "amorously seated in a grotto listening to music." Not only did Tate's scene heighten Edmund's blackness, but it also rendered Regan less credible by allowing her to dally with her lover while her husband is dying, and even to hope that he dies quickly. Garrick shrewdly recognized that the mid-eighteenth-century audience was not likely to be charmed by the Hobbesian instincts of Edmund and would not respond to Tate's mathematical balancing of good against evil characters. He perceived that Tate's dramaturgic plan of action in which the good characters act spontaneously and impulsively whereas the evil characters move with care and deliberation undermined the power of the Shakespearean play.

In addition to deleting portions of Tate's play in order to provide his audience with more robust Shakespearean language and with sharper characterizations, and to rid the play of material offensive to mid-eighteenth-century taste, Garrick also excised lines for purely pragmatic reasons, such as to provide a sharper focus for a scene, or to create a different impact, or simply to expedite stage business.

As a man of practical theatrical instincts, Garrick made the judgment that the public would not easily relinquish all of Tate's *Lear*, the only version of the play, other than his own, that it had witnessed since 1681. He thus retained Tate's happy ending in which Cordelia and Lear are happily united, Cordelia and Edgar assume the rule of the kingdom, and Lear, Gloucester, and Kent retire to the country, "cheered with relation of the prosp'rous reign/ Of this celestial pair" (5.4.159–60).

In addition, Garrick retained the character of Arante, Cordelia's maid, who acts as her confidante. According to Davies, Garrick seriously considered restoring the Fool: "It was once in contemplation with Mr. Garrick to restore the part of the fool, . . . but the manager would not hazard so bold an attempt; he feared . . . that the feelings of Lear would derive no advantage from the buffooneries of the parti-coloured jester."[12]

Garrick's changes in Tate's *Lear* were not made in one step but through a process that has been described as "gradual infiltration" that he was able to accomplish in his multiple roles of playwright, actor, and manager.[13] Although we do not have precise dates on which various changes were made, the most recent research confirms Professor Stone's contention that "from 1747 until the close of his stage career he was giving the play more and more of a Shakespearean flavor."[14] Although Garrick did not make sweeping restorations of Shakespeare in his *Lear*,[15] his version of the play was much closer to Shakespeare's work in spirit, vitality, and scope than what the Restoration and eighteenth-century audiences had seen for almost a century.

## The Tempest (1757)

Garrick had been interested in *The Tempest* since his earliest days as manager of Drury Lane, and he was associated during the span of his career with three different versions of the play: the first, the Dryden-Davenant-Shadwell *Tempest,* which he had presented, to diminishing box-office returns, as late as 1748; the second, his operatic version of the play, which was presented in 1756 and which, despite its fine music, was a theatrical failure; and the third, his adaptation of *The Tempest* as a comedy, which he brought out on October 20, 1757, "As Written by Shakespear." This play bore a closer resemblance to the original Shakespearean text than had any previous Garrick alteration, and it was an immediate and enduring success. It became a permanent part of the repertory and was presented during seventeen of the remaining nineteen seasons that Garrick managed Drury Lane. Garrick's *Tempest* has been described by Stone as "one of the very best of the Shakespearean texts of the eighteenth century."[16]

Given the insights of his acting experience and his overall sensitivity to playhouse potential, Garrick recognized the innate theatricality of Shakespeare's original *Tempest,* with its spectacular opening storm scene, its magical and supernatural ambience, its elaborate masque, and its abundant music. Indeed, the best adaptation for the eighteenth-century audience proved to be no adaptation at all—Garrick presented the play virtually in its original purity. There were few substitutions of language to appease contemporary taste and the deletions that were made—only 432 lines from the entire play—were made only to effect a better acting text.

Garrick did not succumb to the temptation to make any spectacular additions to *The Tempest,* as he had in some of his earlier restorations. Realizing that the play is structured on a minimal plot which focuses on the love of Ferdinand and Miranda and which is given dimension by the subplot of the two conspiracies, Garrick took pains to allow nothing to detract from the characterizations of the lovers and of Prospero, who unites these three motifs.

To emphasize the stature, seriousness, and stateliness of the Magician, Garrick restored nine lines of his well-known fourth-act passage following the masque:

> Our revels now are ended. These our actors,
> As I foretold you, were all spirits and

Are melted into air, into thin air;
And like this unsubstantial pageant faded,
The Cloud-capt towers, the gorgeous palaces,
The solemn temples, the great globe itself,
Yea, all which it inherit, shall dissolve,
And, like the baseless fabric of a vision,
Leave not a rack behind!

(4.1.104–12)

In retaining this passage, Garrick retained one of Shakespeare's favorite metaphors likening life to a play, words appropriate to the good magician. However, he cut two succeeding lines, which are even better known, perhaps fearful that they in their familiarity would detract from the metaphor:

We are such stuff
As dreams are made on, and our little life
Is rounded with a sleep.

Similarly, Garrick's *Tempest,* unlike other adaptations, allowed for the complexity of Caliban's character, retaining for him one of the loveliest passages in the play, his "Be not afraid; the isle is full of noises" speech.

A final strength of Garrick's *Tempest* was the restoration of the original songs. Realizing that the original *Tempest* contained more songs than any other play in the Shakespearean canon, Garrick determined to present every one of them, expanding only one, "Honor, riches, marriage-blessing" sung by Juno in the fourth-act masque. Further, he added no non-Shakespearean songs. As an indication of their importance, the songs were printed and distributed gratis in the theater on opening night.

Garrick had managed to please his audience as well as to restore almost pure Shakespeare. The play was performed sixty-one times before his retirement and was chosen twenty times for actors' benefit performances, when a crowd-pleasing bill was essential. Although Garrick had been severely disappointed at the failure of the operatic *Tempest* the previous year, he could now, with justification, feel that appropriate tribute was being paid to the god of his idolatry.

## *Cymbeline* (1761)

Unlike Garrick's 1759 production of *Antony and Cleopatra* which failed and was withdrawn after only six performances, *Cymbeline* was a great success. Shakespeare's romance was a happy choice of play for Garrick to adapt, for it gave him a light, fanciful plot and the exotic, romantic setting of historic Britain in a Shakespearean work that was not well known to the playhouse audience. In addition, Garrick realized that the dramatis personae included the substantial and appealing roles of Posthumus, the virtuous, courtly husband, and Imogen, his loving, faithful, and courageous wife. Moreover, the role of Iachimo, the repentant villain, and the character roles of Cymbeline, King of Britain, and Bellarius, the knight whom he had banished, gave members of the Drury Lane troupe ample opportunities to display their varied talents.

The world of Shakespeare's *Cymbeline* offers light theatrical fare designed to entertain the viewer without causing him anguish. The tale of the king of ancient Britain, Cymbeline, and the separation and recovery of his family, is informed by two separate plots: the banishment and subsequent adventures of Posthumus, who incurs the king's disfavor because he has married his beauteous only daughter, Imogen; and the loss of his two infant sons years earlier. In Shakespeare's large and somewhat unwieldy play the two plots interrelate just before the end and all concludes happily in a scene of discovery and reconciliation.

The action moves rapidly in Shakespeare's play and the scenes change readily from Britain to Rome and back. Watching the rapid-fire progression of places and events, the viewer always has his attention directed onward toward the final scene. Although there is evil, villainy, and boorishness in the preceding acts, none of it is profound and none of it seems to cause extraordinary pain. The audience responds to the fact that the lovers are reunited and justice has been wrought in the last act.

**Earlier adaptations: D'Urfey's *Injured Princess*.**   Thomas D'Urfey's adaptation of *Cymbeline*, entitled *The Injured Princess, or The Fatal Wager* (1682), substitutes graphic Restoration coarseness for the folktale variety of wickedness of the Shakespearean play. In addition, D'Urfey renames several characters so as to give the play a French flavor. D'Urfey follows the basic Shakespearean plot, but he makes significant changes and additions. Pisanio, the faithful servant of

Posthumus who believes in Imogen's innocence and helps her to flee the court, loses his protective role in the adaptation and is willing to accept Imogen's guilt without question. In addition, the Restoration penchant for balancing characters leads D'Urfey to create a subplot in which Clarina, a daughter of Pisanio, is suspected of helping Imogen, herein named Eugenia, to flee the court, and is, therefore, allowed to be kidnapped by Cloten and his drinking companion and to be raped as punishment. This attack takes place on stage. Somehow, all ends happily in the fifth act, except that Cloten's sinister behavior is fully described at this otherwise joyful scene.

D'Urfey's *Cymbeline* was a moderate success, but Shakespeare's world as rendered by D'Urfey is coarsened, updated, and bereft of its romance.

**Hawkins's adaptation.**    William Hawkins, a professor at Oxford, adapted *Cymbeline* to the neoclassical taste in 1759 by imposing a regular form on the play through observing the unities of time and place, the unity of place mandating the most radical changes. Hawkins' plot borrows at least as much from D'Urfey as from Shakespeare.

Although he did not revive Shakespeare's play, Hawkins provided an entertaining, substantially rewritten version of it. He preserved some of Shakespeare's finest poetry, such as the dirge for Imogen, and had it set to music by the accomplished composer, Dr. Thomas Augustine Arne. Despite its inventiveness and despite the charm invested in Hawkins's *Cymbeline* by the fanciful fourth and fifth acts, the play was not a theatrical success. Genest expressed his measured enthusiasm for the play: ". . . some of Hawkins' additions are far from bad, but the similarity between them and the original play is not very discernible. . . ."[17]

**Garrick's *Cymbeline*.**    In rendering Shakespeare's play, Garrick did not violate the original plot nor did he alter any of the character emphases. He did, however, rearrange some scenes to create an effective eighteenth-century vehicle. For instance, he ends his second act dramatically with two important developments, Imogen's discovery of the loss of her bracelet and her dismissal of the attentions of Cloten by telling him the meanest garment worn by Posthumus is dearer to her than Cloten is, events that are buried in Shakespeare's second act. In the same manner Garrick obtains an interesting effect in reordering the fourth act so as to close it with Lucius's acceptance of Imogen as Fidele, his page. Garrick thus heightens the goodness of Imogen, a trait he knew would find favor with eighteenth-century audiences who were responsive to feminine goodness in the sentimental heroines they applauded nightly.

Another technique used by Garrick is the combining of acts; he renders acts 2 and 3 of the Shakespearean play as his second act. This was largely a practical decision, the response of an eighteenth-century playwright to the requirements of the eighteenth-century stage, one which did not accommodate scene changes as readily as the Shakespearean stage had. Garrick adapted *Cymbeline* so that twenty-six scenes might be performed in only fourteen settings.

Garrick made substantial cuts in the first act, deleting 524 Shakespearean lines. He removed material that might slow the pace of the dramatic action, such as Posthumus's dream and the solution of the riddle. Thus audience attention was focused on the joyous elements of revelation and reconciliation.

Garrick also excised lines that might be misunderstood by the audience as having contemporary application and might, therefore, be considered offensive to taste. Such a passage is Bellarius's explanation of his fall from his position as a courtier:

> the art o' th' court,
> As hard to leave as keep; whose top to climb
> Is certain falling, or so slipp'ry that
> The fear's as bad as falling; the toil o' th' war,
> A pain that only seems to seek out danger
> I' th' name of fame and honor; which dies i' th' search,
> And hath as oft a sland'rous epitaph
> As record of fair act.

After the first night's performance, Garrick also removed a four-line passage from the fifth act in which the treachery of Cymbeline's wicked queen is described. Besides the possibility of violating the code of eighteenth-century taste, both passages, if misunderstood as contemporary comments, would have the effect of diverting audience attention from the magical world of *Cymbeline* to the practical world of eighteenth-century public life.

There is perhaps only one cut made by Garrick which seems to rob the Shakespearean play of a positive element. This is the reduction and rewriting of the twenty-four line dirge sung by Guiderius and Arviragus in the Shakespearean play at the burying of Fidele, lines that have long been counted among Shakespeare's loveliest poetry.

Garrick reduced this to a quatrain sung by Arviragus and a two-line rejoinder of Guiderius.

Sometimes, Garrick rewrote a well-placed line to point up a significant moral, as he did in Iachimo's repentance scene in which he eliminated three lines of muscular Shakespearean verse in order to insert: "With heav'n against me, what is sword or shield;/ My guilt, my guilt, o'erpowers me and I yield" (5.3.11–12).

Knowing the enthusiasm of his audience for music and dance and realizing that the effect of the play would be heightened by resplendent costuming, Garrick saw the opportunity to insert a masque into the second act when Cloten serenades Imogen with the lovely aubade, "Hark, Hark, the Lark." He thus provided for a formal and stylized dance involving at least six performers, including the celebrated Guiseppe Grimaldi.

Garrick's *Cymbeline* was one of his most successful restorations of a Shakespearean play in that he was able to present an authentic version to an eighteenth-century audience and allow them to appreciate it in a near-pure state. In the process he realized a fine acting role, that of Posthumus, for himself, playing it twenty-three times between 1761 and 1763. Moreover, the text of Garrick's *Cymbeline* became the standard and most authentic acting text for generations. In addition, the play received critical acclaim by Garrick's contemporaries and their descendants. The intention he had announced as a young man, to bring the glories of Shakespeare to the eighteenth-century stage, was in this instance, almost perfectly realized.

## *Hamlet* (1772)

Perhaps because it is an actor's showcase, *Hamlet,* as a theatrical vehicle, has been shaped more fully by the actors who have gained renown in the title role than have most other plays. Garrick, who was the accepted English Hamlet for a period of thirty-four years, from his first performance of the role in 1742 until his retirement in 1776, stood strongly in this tradition. As a young actor, Garrick saw himself as a serious student of Shakespeare and, as such, consulted with the leading Shakespearean authorities of the day, including William Warburton and Samuel Johnson. Finding the acting text that had been in use since 1718, the Hughes-Wilks alteration, unsatisfactory in many particulars, he began to revise it as he played the role. His alteration of *Hamlet* was published in 1763 and contains a number of minor cuts and revisions that tightened the action and made the play move more quickly. The 1751 alteration of *Hamlet,* which is very similar to Garrick's 1763 edition, did not bear Garrick's name on the title page but is probably his.

Garrick had, however, another vision of *Hamlet* which he was reluctant to foist on an unwilling public. He waited for a propitious moment and then, encouraged by George Steevens and John Hoadly, presented an alteration of *Hamlet* that eliminated the carnage of the fifth act. Garrick's 1772 alteration of *Hamlet* enraged his critics, delighted his public, and remains the most controversial of his adaptations.

**Earlier adaptations of *Hamlet*.**    The first great Hamlet of the Restoration, Thomas Betterton, acted the play from Davenant's 1661 alteration of a 1637 quarto. Davenant did not rewrite *Hamlet,* but merely cut the play by some eight hundred lines, thus eliminating many significant passages. Among the omissions are Claudius's lines on the state of government, Polonius's advice to Laertes, Hamlet's advice to the players, Rosencrantz's flattery of Claudius, Hamlet's soliloquy "O that this too solid flesh would melt," the advice of both Polonius and Laertes to Ophelia, the mouse-trap, and the Queen's closet scene. In the opinion of Odell, "Altogether, this version is not a bad acting edition . . . the story is compressed to good dramatic effect."[18]

But for Robert Wilks, the next renowned Hamlet, who played the role from 1708 until 1732, the "story" was not sufficiently Shakespearean. He thus engaged the services of the playwright, John Hughes, to restore many of the lines that Davenant had cut. The Wilks-Hughes adaptation, published in 1718, restored such passages as Hamlet's first-act "Angels and Ministers of Grace defend us" lines and his speech to the players, "Speak the speech I pray you." This became the standard acting text for the play until 1772, although sometimes acted with minor changes such as those in the 1751 and 1763 alterations.

**Garrick's *Hamlet*.**    Writing to Suzanne Necker, the wife of the Finance Minister of Louis XVI, who was in London with her husband to see Garrick act in the spring of 1776, Garrick provides a guide to the *Hamlet* he will act the next day. He writes: "the Copy of the play you have got from the Bookseller will mislead You without some direction from Me"; nevertheless, he never allowed the publication of his 1772 alteration. He explains to her how he restructured the first four acts, cut most of the fifth, and added lines of his own: "The first act which is very long in the original is by me divided into two acts—the third act, as I act it, is the second in the original—the third in the original is the fourth in mine, and ends with the famous scene between Hamlet and his mother—and the fifth act in my alteration consists of the fourth and fifth of the original with some small alterations, and the omission of some scenes, particularly the Grave-diggers."[19] The most radical change comes in the fifth act, which concludes without the usual carnage. James Boaden who witnessed Garrick's *Hamlet* in his youth, describes the fifth act thus:

He cut out the voyage to England, and the execution of Rosencrantz and Guilderstern. . . . He omitted the funeral of Ophelia, and all the wisdom of the prince, and the rude jocularity of the grave-diggers. Hamlet bursts in upon the King and his court, and Laertes reproaches him with his father's and his sister's death. The exasperation of both is at its height, when the king interposes; he had commanded Hamlet to depart for England, and declares that he will no longer bear this rebellious conduct, but that his wrath shall at length fall heavy on the prince. "First," exclaims Hamlet, "feel you mine"; and he instantly stabs him. The queen rushes out imploring the attendants to save her from her son. Laertes, seeing treason and murder before him, attacks Hamlet to revenge his father, his sister, and his King. He wounds Hamlet mortally, and Horatio is on the point of making Laertes accompany him to the shades, when the prince commands him to desist, assuring him that it was the hand of Heaven, which administered by Laertes "that precious balm for all his wounds." We then learn that the miserable mother had dropt in a trance ere she could reach her chamber door, and Hamlet implores for her "an hour of penitence ere madness end her." He then joins the hands of Laertes and Horatio, and commands them to unite their virtues (a coalition of ministers) "to calm the troubled land." The old couplet, as to the bodies, concludes the play.[20]

In addition to cutting most of Shakespeare's fifth act, Garrick restored in the first four acts some six hundred lines of the original Shakespearean play that had been cut since Davenant's 1661 alteration. These restorations include the first-act scene in which Cornelius and Voltimand are sent to Norway as ambassadors, as well as references to Fortinbras. The use of these minor characters helps to establish the complex ambience of the court, as Stone has observed: "The subordinate characters become something more than mere puppets to start the show going."[21] Later restorations are of forty-three lines of advice spoken by Polonius to both Ophelia and Laertes, as well as the entire speech of the Ghost. Although Garrick followed the Wilks-Hughes text in omitting the dumb show, the Mouse-Trap play was restored entire, as well as the lines of Claudius, Rosencrantz, and Guildenstern, plotting to send Hamlet to England. The king's whole prayer and Hamlet's reaction are retained, and many lines are restored to Gertrude's closet scene.

The result of the restorations in the first four acts was a keener penetration of the characters surrounding Hamlet, as well as a focusing on the emotional upheavals in the young Prince himself. Davies notes: "The plotting scenes between the King and Laertes, to destroy Hamlet, were entirely changed, and the character of Laertes rendered more estimable."[22] Garrick seemed fascinated with Polonius and he probed unrelentingly the effects of guilt on Claudius. The full scenes dealing with the king's prayer and Hamlet's response to it and his troubled conversation with Gertrude in her closet offer vivid dramatic evidence of his emotional upset. Stone notes: "With the exception of Osric and the gravediggers (who are out), every character in the play is made richer by the restorations."[23]

One problem caused by the new fifth act is that it left Ophelia wandering in a distracted state and the audience unsatisfied about her fate. However, it eliminated the low-comedy gravediggers' scene and solved the problem caused by the rapid succession of scenes in which a frenzied Hamlet leaves Ophelia's funeral, soon to reenter, cocky in his apt disposal of Rosencrantz and Guildenstern. It also allowed for the death of Gertrude by report and satisfied the eighteenth-century penchant for moral uplift in the closing lines of the play in which Hamlet, who has just run upon Laertes' sword and fallen, asks Horatio not to draw his sword in vengeance.

Garrick's *Hamlet* was a brilliant success, holding the stage at Drury Lane until he retired. Although most later critics have been negative in viewing his adaptation,[24] his playhouse audiences were more than enthusiastic. The *London Chronicle* of December 17–19, 1772, reports on a performance of *Hamlet* that Garrick played to a "crouded house," "with uncommon spirit," concluding: "In short, the play makes a very respectable figure in its present state, and the alterations seem to have been produced by the hand of a master." The *Westminster Magazine* for 1773 is even more enthusiastic: "The tedious interruptions of this beautiful tale no longer disgrace it; its absurd digressions are no longer disgusting"; finally, the reviewer, for the December, 1772, *Macaroni and Theatrical Magazine,* comments: ". . . in short, instead of the critical part of the audience being obliged to deduct, the absurdities and improbabilities of this piece from its real merits, the chain of entertainment is now conducted, unbroken and connected."[25]

Garrick, whose characterization of Hamlet on stage had always been marked by subtlety and intelligence, had now a vehicle that allowed him greater scope for psychological penetration, the theatrical gift which was distinctly his, and he was genuinely pleased. Writing to the Abbe André Morellet on January 4, 1773, he says: "I have play'd the Devil this Winter, I have dar'd to alter Hamlet, I have thrown away the gravediggers, & all y^e 5th Act, & notwithstanding the Galleries were so fond of them, I have met with more applause than I did at five & twenty—this is a great revolution in our theatrical history, & for w^ch 20 years ago instead of Shouts of approbation, I should have had y^e benches thrown at my head—my vanity is greatly flatter'd by y^e Event, I never play'd so well in my Life. . . " He concludes his exuberant account of his success with a line from the *Aeneid: "Ceastus artemque repone,* Here victorious I lay down my gauntlet and my art."[26]

## *Katharine and Petruchio* (1754) and *Florizel and Perdita* (1756)

Two slight plays, one presented in March, 1754, and the second in January, 1756, were born of the same impulse: to provide light, diverting entertainment at the same time that the dramatist attempted to communicate as much Shakespeare to the audience as possible. *Katharine and Petruchio,* derived from *The Taming of the Shrew,* was originally written as a benefit for Mrs. Pritchard and soon became the most popular farcical afterpiece on the stage. It remained popular through the nineteenth century. *Florizel and Perdita,* derived from *The Winter's Tale,* was originally written to accompany *Katharine and Petruchio* as a two-part offering. It was a durable theater piece and had a creditable record of performances until May, 1774. When it did not function as a mainpiece to *Katharine and Petruchio,* it served as a conventional afterpiece.

In creating these two successful short plays Garrick used the same basic techniques he had employed in full-length plays. He quickened the pace of action on stage by interrupting long speeches so that they were rendered as conversations by characters who were interacting; he added only as much expository material as was necessary for clarity of plot; he excised much of Shakespeare's gusty language; and, most important, he focused on the disparate farcical moments in the play.

Although markedly different from their predecessors, they effected at least a partial restoration of their originals to the eighteenth-century stage.

## Chapter Five

# The Playwright and the Art of Adaptation: Non-Shakespearean Adaptations

David Garrick explored many sources in his search for plays that would delight his London audiences and he used whatever means he found effective. One means was the adaptation of dramas by other playwrights; one source was plays reflecting an earlier time. Some had been in the repertory during Elizabethan days; some were of Restoration origin; others were contemporary plays that simply had the flavor of earlier times.

Garrick brought to these plays the same principles and methods that he had used in attaining success as a popular dramatist. Of first importance, he sought a vehicle that provided a good fable out of which he could create interesting situations and original characterizations. Having made his selection, Garrick's approach to the plays of other authors was practical, professional, and incisive: he rearranged segments, made appropriate emendations, wrote some sparkling additions, deleted unnecessary scenes, and dropped insignificant characters.

In his adaptations, as in his original plays, Garrick maintained the highest respect for the form of the play, insisting upon taut individual scenes that move sequentially toward a logical climax, with a maximum of dramatic economy. His aim was to present a lively, fast-moving play that would capture, as closely as possible, the spirit of the original. The results of his prodigious energy were new productions of fourteen works by other playwrights, successfully rewritten by Garrick to appeal specifically to the playhouse audience in his time.

The "inextricable combination in him of playwright and actor," which Stone has observed, was another factor clearly evident in Garrick's technique of alteration.[1] He delighted in rewriting that would make the play a better acting vehicle. He reshaped important older plays in order to focus more sharply on a central characterization, as in the case of the rewritten part of Abel Drugger in *The Alchemist* and the new emphasis given Sir John Brute in *The Provok'd Wife*. With his capacity for picking up the nuances of audience preference, Garrick knew that his playgoers relished good-natured spoofing of actors and actresses. Thus he wrote those elements into his adaptation of *The Rehearsal*.

Garrick displayed the same zeal for authenticity in his non-Shakespearean adaptations as he did in those of the Bard. In some adaptations, therefore, he saw himself as a play-doctor, making incisions and simply removing material that was theatrically unproductive. In *Isabella,* for instance, he revised the play by removing the subplot of the original, thus making it a weeping tragedy. In other works, particularly those adapted from the contemporary stage, his alterations were chiefly rhetorical, as he improved the language and removed unnecessary passages to speed up dramatic action and move to an exciting climax.

In other instances Garrick chose a play because of its promising seminal situation but found that considerable rewriting was necessary in order for this situation to be effectively directed toward his particular audience. Thus *The Provok'd Wife,* one of his most popular productions, was markedly altered. Here he sharpened the character contrasts between husband and wife and removed references to religion that might be considered offensive in mid-eighteenth century.

In his multiple roles of playwright, actor, manager, poet, and eighteenth-century gentleman, Garrick had developed a discriminating sense of eighteenth-century London taste. He often found it necessary to delete language that his patrons might find offensive, or to remove situations that were highly topical in earlier times but were of little interest to his contemporaries. He relished opportunities to appeal to the public fancy of the moment by accommodating their increasing love of music or their preference for laughing comedy over sentimental comedy, and he often included these elements in his adaptations.

His alterations are revealing of Garrick the dramatist in that the playwright exercised in these works his well-defined view of what a play should be, in much the same way as he did in his original writings. In all his works he leaned upon his predecessors in the craft of playwriting in his indefatigable search for promising material for stage production. In his adaptations he simply leaned more heavily on his sources than he did in his original works. But both his original works and his alterations show the expert hand of a practiced and professional playwright seeking to delight his audience at the same time that he elevated their taste.

Because the fullest appreciation of Garrick's talents as an adapter of diverse plays drawn from different periods can be had through a comprehensive analysis of selected works, we have chosen to examine in detail one work from each period and to relate other alterations from that same period to it. The three works that we will examine intensively are Garrick's adaptations of Ben Jonson's Tudor composition *Every Man in His Humour* (1598); of Sir John Vanbrugh's Restoration comedy *The Provok'd Wife* (1697); and of Voltaire's neoclassical tragedy *Zaire* (1732), which Garrick renamed *Zara*.

## Adaptations from English Renaissance Plays

From this period Garrick selected Ben Jonson's *Every Man in His Humour*, which became a long-term favorite at Drury Lane; that same author's *The Alchemist* (1612), in which Garrick wholly revitalized the role of Abel Drugger; Thomas Tomkis's *Albumazar* (1615), another humors comedy; the robust comedy of Fletcher and Buckingham, *The Chances;* and James Shirley's *The Gamesters* (1637), which had already been altered early in the century by Charles Johnson.

*Every Man in His Humour.*   Garrick's version of the Jonsonian comedy, which was presented at Drury Lane on November 29, 1751, and published in 1752, was a successful theater piece, preserving for eighteenth-century audiences the antic spirit of the original. Garrick was quick to recognize the comedy inherent in Kitely's discomfiture due to his jealousy of his innocent wife and decided to heighten the impact of this situation by eliminating much of Jonson's low comedy, thus focusing attention more sharply on Kitely.

Jonson's play had originally been acted in 1598 and it is likely that Shakespeare himself was one of the performers. But there is little specific information on performances during Tudor and Elizabethan times and correspondingly little information on specific performances during the Restoration, although we are certain that the play was given and was well received.[2] In fact, little information exists on any production of *Every Man in His Humour* before David Garrick's alteration of the play was performed in 1751. For that production there was great enthusiasm and the play became an established part of the repertory.

In Hogsden, a conservative and comfortable area north of London's wall, Kitely, the merchant, suffers acute discomfiture because of his anxiety that his beautiful young wife might be unfaithful to him. He is further disturbed that Dame Kitely's rascally brother, Wellbred, who lodges with them and uses the house as a meeting place for his group of riotous but harmless young men, will weaken his stature as a merchant. In addition, he does not fancy the possibility that Wellbred's friends, all handsome young men, may have designs on his wife.

One of these friends is Edward Knowell, a young man with an appetite for fine poetry and mirth-making, who gives his father, a sensible and substantial citizen, cause for alarm. Another is Bobadill, one of Jonson's great comic creations, a boasting, swaggering soldier who is likable beneath his cloak of affectation.

The Kitely plot and the Knowell subplot, which embody the actions of the two humors characters, are united by Brainworm, the elder Knowell's wily servant. After a series of episodes involving devices and disguises masterminded by Brainworm, Kitely and his wife meet at the house of Cob, which they mistakenly believe to be a house of ill repute, each one thinking that the other has come for immoral purposes. In the end, Bobadill is exposed and thrashed; young Knowell is married to Dame Kitely's sister; Brainworm is forgiven by Knowell; and all married couples are reconciled to each other and the day's activities. Justice Clement, who has unraveled the mysteries of the day, dedicates the evening to celebration and good fellowship.

In altering *Every Man in His Humour* Garrick attempted to preserve the major characterizations, the intricacies of plot, and the robust comedy of the Jonsonian play. In his "Advertisement" to the printed play he explained his changes and begged the indulgence of his readers: "It is hoped the Liberty that is taken with this celebrated play of *Ben Jonson,* in leaving out some Scenes, with several Speeches and Parts of Speeches in other Places and in adding what was necessary for Connexion, and a whole Scene in the fourth Act, will be excused; as the Distance of 150 Years from the Time of Writing it, had oc-

casioned some of the Humour to be too obsolete, and dangerous to
be ventur'd in the Representation at present." Garrick's description
of his alteration is an accurate statement of a practical operation.

His chief contribution to the play is the improvement of the work
as an acting vehicle. He accomplished this mainly by sharpening the
focus on Kitely's jealousy of his young wife. Garrick realized that
Jonson's play, a very busy work with a long list of characters representing one or another humor, might lose its force through having no
fixed point of interest. He, therefore, expanded the role of Kitely and
Dame Kitely and rearranged Jonson's material so that he, in effect,
wrote a new scene in the fourth act. He also cut the dialogue of ancillary characters, thereby lessening their importance. His changes
had the result of softening the harshness of the humors approach,
which could no longer engage the imagination of a theater audience.

In his rearrangement of the scenes of the fourth act Garrick attained the maximum visual impact by having Kitely remain on stage
continuously. Rather than begin the rewritten scene on a low emotional plane, as Jonson does, by having Kitely reprimand the inter-
loper, Wellbred, for disturbing the peace of his house, Garrick
plunges right into Kitely's problem by a demonstration of his jealousy. Kitely is anxiously questioning his faithful servant, Cash, with
whom he has been searching his home for young Knowell, whom he
believes is secreted there: "Art thou sure, Thomas, we have pried into
all and every part throughout the house? Is there no byplace or dark
corner has escaped our searches?" (4.3.1–3). Assured that Knowell is
nowhere to be found, Kitely vows: "I'll cleanse my house from 'em,
if fire or poison can effect it.—I will not be tormented thus.—They
gnaw my brain and burrow in my heart.—I cannot bear it" (4.3.13–
16). When Cash, fearing that Kitely has agitated himself to the point
of danger, suggests that he call for medical assistance, Kitely responds: "I am not sick, yet more than dead; I have a burning fever
in my mind and long for that which, having, would destroy me"
(4.3.26–28).

When Kitely hears laughter outside, unaware that it is Wellbred
and the ladies laughing at Sir Formal, he believes it is Dame Kitely
and her lover laughing at him because "they have deceived the wit-
tol." Garrick later writes a domestic confrontation into the scene, as
Kitely suggests to Dame Kitely that she stay home more often.
When this idea fails to gain acceptance, Kitely proposes that he accompany her in order to "stop the tongue of slander;/ Nor will I more

be pointed at as one/ Disturbed with jealousy" (4.3.142–44). To Dame Kitely's immediate and stinging question, "Why, were you ever so?" Kitely responds: "What! Ha! never, never—ha, ha, ha!/ (Aside.) She stabs me home.—Jealous of thee!/ No, do not believe it—" (4.3.146–48). He then enters into a lengthy denial, in which he touches upon a variety of emotions, before leaving in search of Cob. Arthur Murphy commented on the effectiveness of this moment, as Garrick played Kitely: "To disguise his suspicions, he assumed an air of gaiety, but under that mask the corrosions of jealousy were seen in every feature. Such was the expression of that various face, that the mixed emotions of his heart were strongly marked by his looks and the tone of his voice."[3] When Kitely learns from Wellbred and Bridget that his wife has gone with Cash to Cob's house, which he believes to be a house of ill repute, his misery is consummate:

> (Aside). So, so; now 'tis too plain. I shall go mad
> With my misfortunes; now they pour in torrents.
> I'm bruted by my wife, betrayed by my servant,
> Mocked at by my relations, pointed at by my neighbors,
> Despised by myself. There is nothing left now
> But to revenge myself first, next hang myself,
> And then—all my cares will be over. (4.3.249–55).

This scene is one of the great comic moments of the play.

Another great moment occurs in 5.4 and might well escape detection by a twentieth-century reader who relies wholly on the written text, failing to visualize the play in performance. In the interview between Justice Clement and Dame Kitely the wife explains that she went to Cob's house because she heard that her husband was there and believed it to be an evil house. Arthur Murphy narrates Garrick's playing the scene as Kitely: " *'Did you find him there'* says the *Justice.* In that instant Kitely interposes, saying, in a sharp eager tone, *'I found her there.'* He who remembers how Garrick uttered those words, slapping his hand on the table, as if he made an important discovery, must acknowledge, trifling as it may now be thought, that it was a genuine stroke of nature."[4]

In addition to writing this scene, which dramatizes Kitely's acute jealousy, Garrick found another way to focus attention on the merchant and his dame. He simply reduced the low comedy, particularly those episodes involving Cob, and cut a substantial number of lines from Matthew and some few lines from the braggart, Bobadill. Because he wanted to retain the flavor of the original play, Garrick chose not to eliminate any characters, but simply to reduce the unwieldy length of the play by shortening the parts of the various minor characters.

In order to make the clearest dramatic progress the playwright also removed all topical allusions that could no longer be savored by the eighteenth-century audience, such as a reference to an Elizabethan place, the slum, Pict-Hatch; and one to an Elizabethan celebrity, the publisher John Trundle. Similarly, allusions to everyday Elizabethan life, and to topical matters of interest to a seventeenth-century audience alone, were excised.

In another effort to maintain the authenticity of Jonson Garrick preserved Jonson's language, unless a change was demanded to insure clarity or to observe eighteenth-century grammatical practice, or to explain a Jonsonian word that had undergone etymological development. There was little in the original play that Garrick deemed offensive or coarse to his eighteenth-century patrons.

In his "Advertisement" Garrick had described the additions to the play as "what was necessary for Connexion," and this characterizes the slight additions of words in the first three acts as well as the rearrangement of material to form a new scene in the fourth act. He also made minor changes to improve the play as an acting vehicle, writing short lines to break a long speech or to provide action or speech for otherwise mute or inactive characters on stage.

Garrick's intimate familiarity with staging practices had mandated changes to reduce the number of scenes and sets required. He reduced the number of scenes by more than fifty percent, from thirty-three to sixteen, a distinct and practical staging advantage in a theater which used extensive scenery and in which a change of scene was, therefore, infinitely more complicated than in Jonson's theater.

Garrick took extraordinary pains to make the play stageworthy, for he was keenly aware of the difficulties involved. In a letter to the Earl of Holderness he expressed some of his reservations about the ability of his company to do justice to the idiom of the Jonson play: "The Language & Characters of Ben Jonson (and particularly of the Comedy in question) are much more difficult than those of any other Writer, & I was three years before I durst venture to trust the Comedians with their Characters, when it was first reviv'd."[5]

Writing of the problems of language Garrick faced in adapting Jonson's play, Thomas Davies observed: ". . . the antiquated phrase of old Ben appeared so strange and was so opposite to the taste of the audience, that he [Garrick] found it no easy matter to make them relish the play. However, by obstinate perseverance, and by retrenching every thing that hurt the ear or displeased the judgment, he brought it at last to be a favourite dramatic dish, which was often presented to full and brilliant audiences."[6]

Garrick had not rewritten Jonson's play to suit the temper of his own times; rather, he had attempted to preserve the form and flavor of the original to the extent to which it was possible. His costuming of the play underscored his theory of adaptation: he insisted that the company be "dress'd in the old English Manner." Garrick's success in preserving the Jonsonian essence of the work may be gauged by the comments of the reviewer for *The London Chronicle* (March 31–April 2, 1757), who perceived the play as Jonson's and did not even mention Garrick:

If we consider that this Piece was exhibited in the Year 1598, being near 160 Years ago, it must be allowed that it is a Proof of an uncommon Genius to entertain us at this Time of Day with Ideas and Manners totally obliterated. It shows that the Painter's Pencil must have been faithful to Nature, otherwise we should hardly please ourselves, at present, with Portraits whose Originals are no more; for excepting the Picture of Jealousy in the Drawing of Kitely there is not one Personage in the whole Group known to our modern Critics. Besides, the Business lies so much in what we call middle Life, or perhaps low Life, and in Parts of the Town disgustful to People of Fashion . . . that nothing but the strong Coloring of old Ben could support the Piece.

Garrick himself played the role of Kitely and it became one of his most popular roles; in fact, he received more congratulations and stirred greater excitement in this role than in any other, except those of Shakespeare. Critics were so enthusiastic about his performance that there was scarcely room for a dissenting opinion. The critic for the *Public Ledger* (November 12, 1771) summed up the situation admirably: "Mr. Garrick's original excellence in the Part of Kitely is universally known, and generally admired." In writing of Garrick's performance as Kitely, the perceptive critic Thomas Wilkes noted his interrelated excellences as writer and actor: "How beautifully does he

paint the jealousy of common life in Kitely. . . . The anxiety and
fears here natural to the part, and the awkward endeavour at disguising the ruling passion, are capital, both in the poet and the
player. . . ."7 Even Horace Walpole, who seldom praised Garrick,
admitted that his performance as Kitely was "as capital and perfect as
action could be."8

Garrick's adaptation of Jonson's "old comedy," was an artistic,
critical, and popular success, encouraging the playwright, still in the
early stages of his career, to recapture and restore additional plays
from earlier glorious periods of the English theater for the delight of
his audience.

## Other Renaissance Adaptations

*The Alchemist.*    Garrick's successful alteration of *Every Man in
His Humour* might well have been predicted by those members of the
audience who had witnessed his earlier alteration of another Jonsonian
comedy, *The Alchemist,* which he had begun to reshape as early as
1743, on first undertaking the role of Abel Drugger. Garrick cut almost one-third of Jonson's comedy of Subtle, the alchemist, who, in
union with his consort, Dol Common, and his friend, Face, plans to
delude and cheat all the gullible folk he can entrap by offering them
the promise of the philosopher's stone. In cutting the text Garrick
reduced the playing time and, by eliminating unnecessary events and
lengthy passages of dialogue, he managed to speed the dramatic action and increase the suspense of the plot.

In addition, he added thirty-three lines to the part of Abel Drugger, the young tobacconist who falls victim to the scheme, thus
sharpening his characterization through a heightening of his naiveté.
Abel Drugger became a more significant character whose stage business was increased and who was thereby afforded opportunities for
visual comedy that were not in Jonson's original work. In Garrick's
alteration of the play the role of Abel Drugger, which the actor chose
for himself and in which he became celebrated, became the focal
point of the play.

In this, his first venture in play adapting, Garrick established his
objective in reshaping plays: to render the play viable in his contemporary theater. Thus he cut words, single lines, sometimes whole passages, that were not absolutely essential to preserve the essence of
Jonson's comedy. In addition, he removed all references to matters of

topical interest to the seventeenth century, but of little interest to the eighteenth-century Londoner, such as allusions to alchemy, Puritanism, and to persons and events of Jonson's time. Additional changes in diction were made to cut references to London whores and seventeenth-century sexual practices that might prove offensive to Garrick's audience. In summary, he reshaped but did not rewrite Jonson's play. By simply cutting material from the original, he preserved Jonson and succeeded in having his audiences applaud Jonson, the playwright, not Garrick, the play-doctor.

*Albumazar.* Garrick altered another play that was close to *The Alchemist* in theme and tone, Thomas Tomkis's *Albumazar*. In October, 1773, he refashioned the text to present it as an example of laughing comedy, a type that had been revitalized by the successful production of Goldsmith's *She Stoops to Conquer* the previous spring. In a Prologue newly written for the 1773 revival Garrick established the similarity of Goldsmith's Tony Lumpkin and the Trincalo of the evening's play. He assured his audience that no scene would hurt their morals and urged them to laugh heartily.

To provide them the occasion for hearty laughter, Garrick reshaped the play so as to focus the attention of the audience on the comic characterization of Trincalo. He accomplished this objective by following his usual formula for adapting: he reduced the size of the original play, in this case by close to eight hundred lines; he deleted unnecessary dialogue so as to quicken the pace of dramatic action; he removed references that would be significant only to the seventeenth-century audience (for the most part, these were references to astrology); and he removed language that might offend the genteel expectations of eighteenth-century taste. He found it necessary to add about two hundred lines of dialogue in order to connect and clarify his greatly reduced plot.

Once again, Garrick's well-tried formula for play-doctoring had proved successful in offering his Drury Lane audiences the best of dramatic fare not otherwise available to them.

*The Chances.* In the "Advertisement" to his alteration of *The Chances* in 1754 Garrick purported to be interested only in rendering the Fletcher-Buckingham work a more decent play, referring to his alterations as "these necessary though slight additions and alterations." In his adaptation and in several later alterations Garrick made the play completely acceptable to the tastes of the eighteenth century. Perhaps more important, he transformed it into a popular theater piece which was performed twelve times during its first season and was presented for twenty-two additional seasons during the century.

Fletcher's play, originally based on a novel of Cervantes, had been revised by George Villiers, Duke of Buckingham, in 1667 and provided good potential theater fare in its depiction of the trials of Constantia, who is eloping with the Duke of Ferrara, before running into a number of complications, including a second Constantia. She is eventually saved, largely through the efforts of two young Spanish gentlemen, Don John and Don Frederick. Buckingham's contribution to the original play was the rewriting of the fifth act and the consequent elevation in importance of the second Constantia.

In his alteration Garrick utilized the plot elements of Fletcher's play, transferring them to Buckingham's plot structure and adding lines of his own wherever necessary for the sake of clarity or connection. His intent was to recover as much of Fletcher as the new and more workable plot structure would allow. He followed his usual practice of deleting passages not necessary to the advancement of the plot; again he cut moralizing passages, removed words and phrases that would be considered offensive to his contemporaries, and cut references no longer meaningful to his modern audience. In quickening the pace of the action and in clarifying the outlines of the plot he heightened the comic characterization of Don John and used it to transform *The Chances* from an "old comedy" into a laughing comedy certain to please the eighteenth-century theatergoers.

**The Gamesters.** In altering James Shirley's comedy, *The Gamester,* Garrick was attacking what has been called "the grossest of Shirley's plays."[9] The play, which had already been altered by Charles Johnson in 1711, contains plot material dangerously close to unacceptable to the mid-century audience. Garrick perhaps chose too difficult a task for himself in seeking to preserve the original play at the same time that he satisfied the taste of his contemporary patrons. His version, which was presented in 1757 with a superb cast, was only moderately successful. In 1772, when Garrick again presented the play after making additional alterations, it fared only slightly better, attaining thirteen performances.

The plot that Garrick tried to rehabilitate involves the love of Wilding for his ward Penelope, a love which he admits to his wife. His wife arranges for Penelope to meet Wilding and then takes Penelope's place. All goes awry because the gamester, Wilding, then engaged in gambling, sends his friend Hazard, to take his place.

Confusion follows upon confusion, and there are some amusing comic incidents of the manners variety.

In his alteration Garrick removed a comic subplot involving Violante and Leonora to focus attention on the gamester and his ever-worsening plight. He was successful in using Shirley's idiom whenever he made additions, one reviewer noting: ". . . the reader will find no little difficulty to distinguish what is the Alterer's from what is Shirley's; he has so well imitated his stile, and fallen into his turn of thought and expression."[10] In other respects, however, critical reaction was poor among Garrick's contemporaries and later critics, as well. John Genest perhaps best summarizes the critical consensus: ". . . his alteration does him no great credit," adding that ". . . his additions are insipid."[11]

As Garrick's only Elizabethan alteration that did not meet with success, *The Gamesters* serves to remind us of Samuel Johnson's dictum: "The Drama's Laws the Drama's Patrons give." Although Garrick was anxious to restore the vigor of the "old comedy" to the English stage, he could not transcend the boundaries of taste established by his audience.

## Adaptations from English Restoration Plays

Garrick selected three plays from among the works of the most significant playwrights of the period: John Vanbrugh's *The Provok'd Wife* (1697); the Duke of Buckingham's *The Rehearsal* (1671); and William Wycherley's *Country Wife* (1675), which Garrick renamed *The Country Girl*. From this period he also chose two non-comic plays: Dryden's *King Arthur* (1691), which the original author had called a "Dramatick Opera," and which Garrick rewrote and renamed a "Masque," and a tragedy, Thomas Southerne's *The Fatal Marriage; or, The Innocent Adultery* (1694), which Garrick adapted as *Isabella; or, The Fatal Marriage*.

**The Provok'd Wife.**   *The Provok'd Wife* had a magnetic appeal for Garrick as an acting piece because Vanbrugh's 1697 Restoration comedy had retained its popularity for over forty years. Moreover, the play offered a challenge since it had commanded the best histrionic talents available during its long span, from Betterton, Mrs. Barry, and Mrs. Bracegirdle to Charles Macklin and Peg Woffington. In addition, *The Provok'd Wife* had gained a substantial following among the reading public, having gone through nine editions by 1743.

From its earliest days, however, the play had undergone severe criticism because of its unfavorable references to religion and its exploitation of titillating sexual situations. *The Provok'd Wife* was barraged with the heavy artillery of Jeremy Collier's attack in *A Short View of the Immorality and Profaneness of the English Stage* (1698), just one year after its first performance. Bending to the criticism of Collier and other moralists, Vanbrugh agreed to a slight revision of the play. The most significant alteration occurred in a scene in which Sir John Brute, after spending a drunken evening with Lord Rake and Colonel Bully, dons a parson's gown and parades through town in that attire, before being arrested for brawling in the streets. Vanbrugh, in his alteration, substituted Lady Brute's gown for the parson's robe. In addition, the playwright deleted some of Sir John's lines spoken in the guise of a parson, such as "My talent lies towards Drunkenness and Simony" and "Sir—I have—a very good Cure—for the Clap, at your Service."

Although the most offensive references to religion and the person of the clergyman had been removed by Vanbrugh, Garrick realized, as he prepared the role for performance as Sir John Brute in 1744, that the play required substantial tailoring if it were to continue to please audiences, who were becoming more and more fully committed to the moral emphases of sentimental drama. Garrick first played the role of Sir John Brute on November 16, 1744, and repeated the part eight times during the season. He took it up again on November 10, 1747, when he was also manager of Drury Lane and appeared frequently as Sir John Brute until his retirement in 1776. Garrick made many revisions in the play—gradually over a thirty-year period. An early prompt copy used by Garrick, made on a 1743 edition of the play, may have been used for his first appearance in the role. Substantial revisions are printed in Garrick's alteration of 1761, but the fullest picture of his alteration of *The Provok'd Wife* is seen in the 1776 edition, issued just prior to his retirement. In his final reworking of *The Provok'd Wife,* as in his earlier alterations, Garrick was drawn to a comedy of great vitality which seemed eminently suited to theatrical presentation. He attempted to preserve the spirit of the original work, presenting it within the parameters acceptable to his eighteenth-century audience.

Although Vanbrugh's Sir John Brute is not a lovable character, he was always the dramatic center of the play, spewing his churlish abuse upon his long-suffering wife. Though she has been receiving the attentions of Constant, a man-about-town, she has remained faithful to her husband. But her virtue is thrown into jeopardy when she and her niece, Belinda, who is being courted by the once-cynical Heartfree, meet the gentlemen in Spring Garden, at the invitation of the ladies. Fortunately, the four are interrupted by the appearance of Sir John, drunk from his evening's roistering and attired in a lady's robe. Further, Lady Fancyfull, who is drawn by the charms of Heartfree and who has, therefore, followed Constant and Heartfree to Spring Garden in a fit of jealous curiosity, suddenly jumps out of her hiding place and rushes away, causing Lady Brute and Belinda to worry that they have been recognized and to hurry home.

When the two couples, returning to Lady Brute's house, sit down to play cards, they are once again interrupted, again by Sir John Brute, who has been dismissed by the magistrate after having been arrested for brawling. He finds Heartfree and Constant in a closet, but in his drunken state he is not inclined to accept Constant's challenge to a duel. Somehow the mayhem is attributed to the impending marriage of Heartfree and Belinda and, despite the fact that Lady Fancyfull has sworn revenge, all ends happily.

Garrick's first concern in making the play appealing to his audience was to heighten the contrast between Lord and Lady Brute. Vanbrugh's play had suffered from the fact that Lady Brute, because of her frank discussions with her niece on the intricacies of sex and the pleasure of cuckolding her husband, had emerged as only slightly more attractive than her husband. To remedy this and to create a favorable initial impression, Garrick removed most of her first-scene musing on the justification that her husband's behavior gave her for breaking her marriage vow. He also deleted her concluding remark: "Virtue's an ass, and a gallant's worth forty on't." Instead, Garrick's Lady Brute concludes: "I think I have a right to alarm this surly brute of mine—but if I know my heart, it will never let me go so far as to injure him." Lady Brute's character is immediately softened and she enters the ranks of eighteenth-century characters whose essential goodness of heart lessens the force of their subsequent indiscretions.

It is possible to count seventy-seven instances in which Garrick, the adapter, deleted material from Vanbrugh's text. Much of his deletion was intended to strengthen the sympathetic emphasis given Lady Brute's character in 1.1. One such masterful omission occurs in 3.3, where Garrick cuts a lengthy dialogue between Lady Brute and Belinda. The ladies, relaxed and preparing for sleep, exchange opinions on a variety of topics, from the suggestion that men in love look like asses to the fact that rivalry between women is essentially a bid for masculine attention. Vanbrugh's Lady Brute delivers a splendid analysis of the self-conscious flirtatious behavior of ladies at the playhouse as well as a summary of the female dilemma: "If we quit our modesty they say we lose our charms, and yet they know that very modesty is affectation and rail at our hypocrisy." The dialogue contains some sparkling moments and, no doubt, amused the devotees of wit in the Restoration audience, but it characterizes Lady Brute as an affected lady of quality rather than an abused wife.

A similarly effective omission occurs in 5.2, where Garrick cuts fifty lines of dialogue between Lady Brute and Belinda in which Lady Brute caps her discussion of virtue with her analysis of the differences in the ethical behavior of men and women: "Men have more courage than we, so they commit more bold, impudent sins. They quarrel, fight, swear, drink, blaspheme and the like. Whereas we, being cowards, only backbite, tell lies, cheat at cards, and so forth." Both Lady Brute and her niece are revealed in this scene as detached and analytical, impressions that would not serve Garrick's dramatic ends.

Garrick also excised words and phrases offensive to the religious sensibility of the day. He substituted a new song by Colonel Bully for that sung by Vanbrugh's Lord Rake in 3.1 which contained the objectionable lines: "And religion ne'er dares to disturb me," "In peace I've my whore,/ And in peace I jog on to the devil." In 5.3 Garrick deletes part of the dialogue between Constant and Heartfree in which the latter says: "All revolutions run into extremes: the bigot makes the boldest atheist, and the coyest saint the extravagant strumpet."

In addition, Garrick made a number of word substitutions to lessen the force of Vanbrugh's overtly sexual language. In the dialogue between Vanbrugh's Lady Brute and Belinda in 3.3, cited above, Belinda queries Lady Brute:

> Bel:   . . . and sure you would not have me commit fornication.
> Lady B:   . . . if 'twere only to keep me in countenance whilst I commit—you know what.

Garrick's alteration reads thus:

> Bel:   . . . and sure you would not have me do I don't know what with him.

> Lady B: . . . if 'twere only to keep me in countenance whilst I
> play the fool with Constant.

This example is representative of the numerous changes Garrick made to cater to mid-century taste. Among others, he rewrote Vanbrugh's "be damned" as "hang myself"; "possessing a mistress" as "gallanting"; "be lewd" as "be kind"; and "whore on" to "rake on."

Yet Garrick, as playwright, knew well the theatrical value of teasing his audience by bringing them to the very brink of the shocking. The newly written song in 3.3 that he assigned to Colonel Bully, rather than Lord Rake, is, like Vanbrugh's, coarse and vulgar, though it does succeed in omitting references offensive to religion. In addition, Garrick retained the lines Vanbrugh had written for Rasor, Sir John's *valet de chambre,* which is a play upon the word "whoring": "My master's asleep in his chair, and a-snoring:/ My lady's abroad, and—Oh rare matrimony!" Concluding 5.2., the couplet was theatrically effective. Finally, with considerable impunity, Garrick retained Rasor's angry and licentious remark in 5.5 that Lady Fancyfull, in punishment for tempting him, "should lie upon her face all the days of her life."

Consistent with his general practice of alteration, Garrick made some changes in the play for the sake of clarity, such as the removal of topical allusions of Vanbrugh's time, items that would hardly be recognized by a mid-century audience. His elimination of the minor characters, Treble and Pipe, who provided little more than decorative music, helped to speed up the dramatic action. Twice he shifted lines among characters and eight times he shortened lines for the same purpose.

Garrick also had a fine instinct for preserving intact certain scenes of the original play. One of these was Sir John's drunken scene in the fifth act, which Georg Christoph Lichtenberg saw Garrick perform and which he describes with rare enthusiasm in a letter dated October 10, 1775:

> . . . he again breaks into coarse talk, and suddenly becomes so wise and merry in his cups that the whole audience bursts into a tumult of applause. I was filled with amazement at the scene where he falls asleep. The way in which, with shut eyes, swimming head, and pallid cheeks, he quarrels with his wife, and uttering a sound where 'r' and 'l' are blended, now appears to abuse her, and then to enunciate in thick tones moral precepts, to which he himself forms the most horrible contradiction. . . ".[12]

Such a scene heightened Garrick's conception of Lady Brute as the abused wife and served to emphasize her essential goodness. In his alteration he used her dialogues with Belinda to externalize her sufferings, rather than to exploit the battle of the sexes as Vanbrugh had done. Both women were sympathetically presented to Garrick's audience and some sentimental elements appeared in their characterizations. Further, Garrick's removal of references offensive to religion and his softening of the harsh, explicitly sexual language of the Restoration play inclined his audience to accept it.

The history of the play indicates that they accepted it with enthusiasm for the rest of Garrick's career. Moreover, the play was frequently performed at the rival theater at Covent Garden during the same period. In both houses it commanded the top acting talents: at Drury Lane Garrick played the role of Sir John Brute, while Covent Garden offered Cibber, Quin, and Woodward, at different times. Once again, the extraordinary success of a play was due to the combined force of three elements in Garrick's professional makeup: his considerable playwriting skill, his uncanny theatrical acumen which enabled him to anticipate audience response, and his uncommon acting abilities.

**Other Restoration Adaptations.**    Garrick additionally sought to restore two comedies of leading Restoration comic playwrights: Buckingham's *Rehearsal* and Wycherley's *Country Wife*. Restless for new ventures, he also experimented in tragedy, in adapting *Isabella,* and in a musical production, Dryden's *King Arthur.*

Garrick's very successful adaptation of *The Rehearsal* was due to his ability to shift the object of the attack in Buckingham's play from Dryden and the bombastics of heroic tragedy to mid-century playwrights in general. In addition, he deleted references to plays and playwrights of Buckingham's day and updated the mimicry of actors to mock players of his own day. He improved the text, as he had improved the texts of numerous other plays, by quickening the dramatic action and reducing the amount of decorative singing and dancing. As in many of his alterations, Garrick's superb acting of a key part, in this case, Bayes, almost guaranteed the success of the piece.

*The Country Girl,* the title Garrick gave to his alteration of Wycherley's comedy, *The Country Wife,* which he brought out in 1766, achieved sufficient popular success to last for five seasons, but it came at the expense of Garrick's artistic aims. Perhaps having learned from the failure of his adaptation of Shirley's *Gamester* in 1757 that the Drury Lane audience would not tolerate extreme plot situations, he decided it was necessary to rewrite substantive portions of Wycherley's comedy about the trepidations of the elderly Pinchwife and the flirtations of his young wife, Margery. In this instance, he had to gainsay his artistic objective of adhering closely to the original text of an older play. Although he retained the subplot of Sparkish and Alithea, it is cast in a different light and Horner, the witty young libertine who declares himself a eunuch, is removed from the play entirely. In Garrick's alteration the wife becomes a spinster, and the episode of a would-be parson performing a bogus marriage is deleted. Garrick changed the flavor of the play from the comedy of wit to something approaching a romantic comedy, but his critics complained that, in deleting much of the play, he also removed its cleverness and appeal.

*King Arthur; or The British Worthy* was Garrick's first venture in altering a musical play. Dryden's 1691 production had been successful in blending a fable with fine music and glorious spectacle. Garrick intended to achieve the same effect for the audience of his time. In order to do that, he substituted the melodious compositions of Dr. Arne for what now sounded like the old-fashioned, though majestic music of Henry Purcell, and he took advantage of the technical advances that had been made in stagecraft. In the text Garrick made fewer changes from the original than he had in any other alteration. The production captured the public fancy, William Hopkins noting in his Diary for December 13, 1770, after its first performance: "This Masque was got up in a Superb manner," and *King Arthur* was performed twenty-one times during its first season.

Garrick's *Isabella*, his first venture into the adaptation of tragedy, which he brought out in 1757, was even more successful. He chose to alter Thomas Southerne's hoary she-tragedy, *The Fatal Marriage; or, the Innocent Adultery*, a play which had been in performance since its first appearance in 1694, but whose popularity since its last printing in 1735 was on the decline. The opportunities for pathos were obvious in the fable of the beautiful young Isabella, who, believing her husband to be killed in battle, acquiesces to the strong suggestion of his younger brother Carlos, and marries her faithful suitor, Villeroy. When Biron, her husband, returns after seven years and reveals himself to his wife, he is attacked and mortally wounded by the villainous Carlos, who wants to succeed to his position. The distracted Isabella kills herself.

Intending to give the play the full force of weeping tragedy, Garrick cut over one thousand lines from a comic subplot which had been written to please Restoration audiences and which, according to Francis Gentleman, "rendered it gross enough for the entertainment of a brothel."[13] But he retained the main plot almost in its entirety and the few additions that he made are largely developments of characterization, which was his forte in adapting older plays.

Through his adaptations of five significant Restoration plays, Garrick succeeded in allowing his contemporary audience to experience the vitality of the former age in a form which they saw as both entertaining and elevating.

## Adaptations from Contemporary Plays

In selecting works from his own age for alteration Garrick continued to explore the musical and tragic forms. He revived the elaborate musical work of David Mallet and James Thomson, *Alfred* (1740); he rewrote William Whitehead's *Roman Father* (1750) to make it more stageworthy; and he took pains to capture the essence of two works of Voltaire that had been successful on the Paris stage, *Mahomet* (1742) and *Zaire* (1732).

**Zara.** In adapting Voltaire's *Zaire* for Drury Lane Garrick sought to bring the best of contemporary French neoclassical tragedy to an English audience. He was aware that his countrymen had to be enticed into a theatrical experience of any novelty. Since the sustained intensity of French tragedy was foreign to the English stage, Garrick's task as adapter was to preserve the spirit of the original play in a form acceptable to his audience. His genius is that, with supreme regard for the original text, he modified Voltaire's play only insofar as it was necessary to make it an effective theatrical vehicle in England.

Voltaire's *Zaire* was a notable success on the Parisian stage when it was presented in August, 1732, and it was performed thirty-six consecutive nights. Its first great success in London was at Drury Lane in a literate but freewheeling translation by Aaron Hill in January, 1736. Introducing Susannah Cibber as a dramatic actress, the play held the boards for fourteen successive performances. But, after its first flush of success, its popularity dimmed and it was not presented at either of the patent theaters again until 1752 at Covent Garden. In March, 1754, the Irish actor, Mossop, chose the play for his benefit night and Garrick played the role of Zara's father, Lusignan. The performance was very successful and the play became one of the staple items of the Drury Lane repertory until Garrick's retirement, drawing consistently large houses to the theater. After his retirement Garrick's version remained a popular favorite until well into the nineteenth century.

It is likely that, in adapting this play, he followed the same practice he had effected in his alteration of many Shakespearean and non-Shakespearean works: altering his own part on stage for reasons of theatrical effectiveness and, thence, the parts of other characters, over a long period of time. Compared to Hill's overblown translation of *Zaire,* Garrick's was lean and incisive. Although he did not publish the adaptation of this play under his own name, a promptbook in Garrick's hand made upon a 1763 edition of Hill's translation gives us Garrick's alteration of the play.[14]

The attraction of Voltaire's work for Garrick is obvious: a dramatization of elemental passions, the play attains a tragic grandeur through its simplicity. Zaire, the young, beautiful slave of Osman, Sultan of Jerusalem, loves her master wholly and looks forward to becoming his Sultana. But Osman is troubled by the return of Nerestan, a young French gentleman whom he had released from bondage to return to France to seek ransom for the captives of the Sultan, especially Zaire. Osman, impressed with the honor and altruism of the young Frenchman who had agreed, upon his return, to become the Sultan's slave, decides to release all his captives but two: Lusignan, an aged French nobleman who was once Jerusalem's Christian king, and Zaire, whom he loves and plans to marry. When Nerestan betrays his anger, Osman believes the young Frenchman has romantic designs on his future bride. Zaire secures the release of Lusignan, as a pledge of her continuing efforts to help all Christians when she is Sultana.

Lusignan, in recounting his own adventures in battle with Osman, in listening to Nerestan tell the story of his life, and in noticing a particular piece of jewelry worn by Zaire, realizes that he is the father of both Nerestan and Zaire. In a moment of great emotion, under the force of this revelation, Zaire vows to renounce her Eastern lover and announce herself a Christian. Her anguish, as she considers the claims

of her Christian heritage versus her deep love for Osman, is matched
by the suffering of the Sultan, whose jealousy becomes inordinate as
he believes Zaire is spending time with Nerestan and Lusignan because of a romantic involvement with Nerestan. When Osman learns
from a slave that Zaire had wept upon receiving a letter from Nerestan and had agreed to meet him that evening, the Sultan follows her
and, believing himself betrayed, stabs her to death. After learning
from Nerestan, who arrives a few minutes later, that Zaire was his
sister, Osman consumed by despair, orders that all Christians be freed
and stabs himself to death.

The scene in which the aged King Lusignan recognizes Zaire and
Nerestan as his children was a favorite with the audience. Garrick,
playing the role of the old father, used the insights of the actor to
make subtle alterations in the language to heighten the emotional
impact of the scene. He keeps attention squarely on the aged father,
who tries to direct Zaire back to Christianity. Garrick's Lusignan
spurs his children on with the lines: "These are the times, my
friends, to prove our firmness,/ Our Christian firmness." Garrick had
inserted *prove* for the earlier and milder *try*. As playwright, Garrick
also deleted language that failed to attain an immediate and arresting
effect; for it he substituted words and phrases that were rough-hewn
and direct. He removed entire passages that might deflect the audience's attention from the central conflict in the mind of Zaire.
Stripped of all that was weighty, distracting, and counterproductive,
the emotions dramatized on stage were finely chiseled and directly
communicated.

*Zara* offers splendid opportunities for passionate acting and Garrick appreciated its essential theatricality. There was, however, one
significant change that he made in characterization: in order to focus
the audience sympathy solely on Zara, he was painstaking in removing marks of nobility in her lover. He removed from Osman two lines
in which he muses on the role of a monarch and expresses his will-
ingness to see his former slave, Nerestan, recently returned from
France: ". . . Monarchs, like the sun,/ Shine but in vain, unwarm-
ing, if unseen" (1.1.209–10). In that same passage Garrick also cut
two lines in which Osman showed himself sensitive to his subjects:
"I think with horror on these dreadful maxims/ Which harden kings
insensibly to tyrants" (1.1.214–15).

In his alteration Garrick refused to depict Osman primarily as
lover. Thus he cut the line of the Sultan to his minister, "My love is

stronger, nobler than my power" (1.1.275). He was similarly unwilling to have Osman detail his feelings of love for Zara. Finally, he cut Osman's line that indicated his dual devotion to kingship and his beloved: "Zara to careful empire joins delight" (1.1.280), spoken in earlier versions by the Sultan to his confidante, Orasmin. By these and similar cuts, Garrick made Osman a less attractive character and strengthened the likelihood that the sympathetic audience response would be directed to Zara alone.

Throughout the play Garrick deleted many lines to quicken the pace of the whole. Since he usually cut a few lines rather than an entire passage or scene, he was able to retain the essence of the Voltaire play.

In addition to these three most significant kinds of changes: those made to render the character of Osman less sympathetic, those made to delete lines added by Hill which were not in Voltaire's original, and those deletions made to speed up the action, Garrick made a number of less important kinds of changes: he routinely removed references to religion, reduced the number of passages that might be construed as moralizing, and removed some few lines that might be thought to have political implications. In the words of a modern editor, "the result is a play in which the unnaturalness of neoclassical tragedy is reduced by cutting down long speeches, reducing dramatic narration, and breaking up lengthy, yet necessary, speeches with lines for other players; one in which obscure lines are clarified, suspense is maintained where it flagged in Hill's version, and the intent of the original author is restored whenever Garrick felt that the English translator had strayed too far from his text."[15]

The effectiveness of Garrick's alteration was demonstrated by the continuing popularity of *Zara*. Following Garrick's initial appearance in the role of Lusignan, the play was performed every season at Drury Lane until his retirement. Garrick's influence continued, for the Bell editions of 1776, and 1791, and Mrs. Inchbald's of 1808 remain basically Garrick's alteration from his acting copy.[16]

Lusignan became one of Garrick's favorite and most effective roles. On March 7, 1775, more than twenty years after he first played the role, a Dr. Thomas Campbell went to the theater at five o'clock, a full hour before curtain time, to see Garrick, but the crowds were so great he couldn't get a seat.[17] Contemporary accounts record Garrick's effectiveness in supporting his text with a perfection of tone, glance, gesture, and elocution that mesmerized his audience. Even so distinguished a visitor as Jean Jacques Rousseau is said to have told Garrick, after witnessing him in the role on January 23, 1766, that he cried throughout the tragedy.[18]

Garrick's *Zara* on stage and in the many editions that were printed throughout the century attained the highest aims of the playwright-adapter: it refined an important play, presenting it to the contemporary English audience in the manner in which they could best appreciate the intent and genius of the original work.

**Adaptations from Other Contemporary Plays.** Garrick's involvement in the revision of William Whitehead's *Roman Father,* an English play in the French classical tradition, presents detailed evidence of his careful concern in presenting contemporary tragedy in its most effective form. Garrick persuaded the author to accept the working principles he himself had followed in previous alterations: he cut the length of Whitehead's work, thus quickening its dramatic pace; he produced a more rapid climax; and he deleted language that was grandiose and bombastic. The result of these changes, all rhetorical, was a play, produced in 1750, that remained in the repertory for fifty years and prolonged the vogue for plays in the French classical tradition.

Another play in that tradition that attracted Garrick was Voltaire's *Mahomet the Imposter,* which had been brought to the English stage in 1744, within two years of its Paris premiere, through an adaptation made by James Miller and Dr. John Hoadly. Garrick described their work as "partly a translation and partly an imitation." Their version of the play about Mahomet, the cold-blooded villain who delights in his wickedness, attained only middling success until Garrick decided to alter it for presentation at Drury Lane in 1765. He was careful, as Hoadly and Miller had been, to preserve the Voltaire original and his revisions were chiefly rhetorical. He cut unnecessary language, quickened the pace of the action, deleted much of the bombast, and deemphasized the incest theme of the original work. Garrick's educated guess that a fresh production of Voltaire would win the plaudits of his audience in the mid-1760s was accurate. Garrick's *Mahomet* entertained the town and continued as a viable theater piece into the next century.

For his last theatrical adaptation Garrick chose the thirty-year-old masque, *Alfred,* which he presented with all the wonders of spectacle that contemporary stagecraft allowed him. Originally written in 1740 by James Thomson and David Mallet at the request of the Prince of

Wales for private presentation, *Alfred* was redone by Mallet in 1751 for Garrick's appearance in the title role at Drury Lane. The 1751 alteration of the masque, in which Garrick had no hand, had attained moderate theatrical success but was, in Garrick's opinion, inferior to the original work in some respects. Thus, when he himself altered the play for production in 1773, Garrick discarded some of the additions made for the 1751 production and returned to the original. Significantly, he reinstated the original songs, including the authentic, "Rule, Brittania." To give the old masque the strongest advantages of contemporary presentation, Garrick called on de Loutherbourg to design new scenes and he included a spectacular naval review. Finally, he added some new music written by the contemporary composer, Augustus Smith.

Garrick's 1773 *Alfred* was a triumph of eighteenth-century production practices placed at the disposal of the play adapter. Garrick successfully used the technical advantages of his time to present, more lavishly, the richness of the original masque.

## Chapter Six
# Garrick the Occasional Poet

Biographers have noted, with apparent surprise, both the volume and variety of Garrick's poetry. It is surely noteworthy that a man seriously committed to writing plays, whose every other hour was apparently given to the exigencies of acting and managing a theater, wrote over four hundred poems. But it is more remarkable that Garrick, the practical man of affairs and the fastidious organizer, seemed so careless about his poems. George Kearsley, who collected and published Garrick's poetry in 1785, rather fussily noted: "The Author, careless and indifferent about his smaller productions, dispersed them in such a variety of publications, that, had he been now living, he would probably have found some difficulty in assembling them together, or even, without assistance, to recollect them."[1]

This uncharacteristic apparent indifference of Garrick to the details of his life stems, in large part, from the fact that he perceived his writing of poetry as a wholly natural and expected aspect of the life of a sophisticated gentleman. Occasional verse, which in earlier English literature, referred to poems written to adorn or commemorate an important specific event, had become by mid-eighteenth century a flourishing literary activity, with poems written, not only to note specific important moments in the national life, but to recall ordinary moments in the lives of unexceptional people. Numerous poetical miscellanies were published; newspapers and periodicals published much occasional verse too. Those who did not feel sufficiently at ease to communicate in light verse were encouraged to do so in manuals instructing the reader how to write poetry, the manuals themselves selling many copies.[2]

Garrick, as a man of his time, communicated quite naturally in verse. His particular gifts were well suited to occasional verse: sensitivity to the exact choice of words; deft use of the well-turned phrase; the conversational manner; and an urbanely good-humored view of the world.

He used his poetic gifts primarily in writing for the theater: mostly prologues, epilogues, and songs for his own plays and those of others. He also used his poetry as artillery when the situation demanded it, as in his writing "The Fribbleriad," a scathing attack upon Thaddeus Fitzpatrick, who had led a scurrilous paper attack on him, and in penning "The Sick Monkey," written to fend off criticism upon his return to the stage after his 1763 European tour.

In addition to exhibiting his theatrical ventures Garrick's poetry reveals much of his personal life. His poetry on actors and actresses shows a warm regard for their talents and their friendship. Certain poems written to close friends display that same appealing warmth, such as "Written at Hampton," a poem to Colman on his translation of Terence, and the "Sonnet" to the Duchess of Devonshire. Other poetry reveals his status with the celebrities of the day: "On Johnson's Dictionary," "Epitaph on William Hogarth," and "Advice to the Marquis of Rockingham."

Still another flavor is evident in Garrick's epigrams: terse and biting poetry, written with much wit. To his friends, however, he sometimes communicated in merry verse epistles, such as his lines to Richard Rigby entitled "To the Good Folk at Mistley." In his serious moments he rose to the demands of a formal ode, composing one for the Shakespeare Jubilee celebration in 1769 and another to be set to music by different candidates for the Catch Club prize. In one sense, his poetry may be seen as an accurate mirror of his life: polished, sophisticated, moral, pleasing, and earnest, without the affectation of unnecessary complication.

## Poems about the Theater

Garrick's first epilogue dates back to his first play, *Lethe,* written in 1740, and he continued to write prologues and epilogues well into his retirement. Since they give us his perceptions of the most significant issues in the theatrical milieu, they are of immense interest for their content as well as for their esthetic excellence. In an early poem, the "Epilogue" to James Ralph's *Astrologer* (1744), Garrick cleverly creates a sense of camaraderie with his audience by appealing to their patriotic instincts and asserting unequivocally the English superiority over the French:

> A modish frenzy so corrupts the town,
> That nought but *Alamode de France* goes down:
> We all submit to this fantastic yoke,
> Like them we dress, we dance, we eat, we joke;

From top to toe they change us at their will;
All but our hearts—and those are British still.

Garrick returned often to this theme, concerned lest the adulation of
French manners contaminate English taste. In the "Prologue" to *Taste*
(1752), a comedy by Samuel Foote, Garrick, costumed as Peter Puff,
auctioneer, reports to his audience: "'Tis said *Virtu* to such a height
is grown/ All artists are encourag'd—but our own." Characteristically, he challenges the audience to accept its responsibility for excellence in the theater: "If we should fall, to you it will be owing:/
Farewell to Arts—they're going, going, going."

Garrick was not simply challenging his audience, but rather ver-
sifying the problem that was his great preoccupation during the
whole of his managerial tenure at Drury Lane: the challenge of elevating public taste consistent with his view of the contribution theater should make to a civilized society, at the same time that he
provided sufficient entertainment to fill his house nightly, and thus
maintain financial stability. These were the sentiments he voiced as
early as in the "Occasional Prologue," which he spoke at the opening
of the 1750 season:

> Sacred to SHAKESPEARE was this spot design'd,
> To pierce the heart and humanize the mind.
> But if an empty House, the Actor's curse,
> Shews us our Lears and Hamlets lose their force;
> Unwilling we must change the nobler scene,
> And in our turn present you Harlequin.

Garrick also challenged his audience to live decent and moral lives.
That standard always appeared in his plays, seen either directly or in-
directly, and Garrick, the prologuist, amiably teased his audience,
reminding them of their failings. In the "Prologue" to *The Male Coquette; or, Seventeen Hundred Fifty-Seven* he addresses the young men of
fashion in the audience:

> Ye slaves to fashion, dupes of chance,
> Whom Fortune leads her fickle dance;
> Who, as the dice shall smile or frown,
> Are rich and poor, and up and down;

he then speaks to the ladies of fashion:

> Ye ladies too, maids, widows, wives,
> Now tremble for your naughty lives
> How will your hearts go pit-a-pat?

Then, in a characteristic eighteenth-century disclaimer, the prologuist assures the members of the audience that the dramatic characters soon to appear on stage are all fictitious. As George Winchester Stone, Jr., has noted, Garrick's prologues almost always contained a moral,[3] but the moral was delivered with such urbane good humor and was so artfully imbedded in the fabric of the poem that it did not offend.

In addition to writing prologues and epilogues, Garrick wrote a substantial number of songs, most of which are included in his own plays and the plays of other authors. However, a number of songs written independently of specific plays celebrate a patriotic motif, and they are among his most interesting poetry. One, "The lilies of France, and the fair English rose," written in high spirits at the outset of the Seven Years War in 1756, is a rousing ballad, appropriately devoid of subtlety, ending with the lines: "Huzza for Old England, whose strong pointed lance/ Shall humble the pride and the glory of France." The following year Garrick had Dr. Arne set to music the hearty and amusing, "Ye true honest Britons," which is a celebration of beer-drinking Britons:

> Let us sing our own treasures, Old England's good cheer,
> The profits and pleasures of stout British beer;
> Your wine-tippling, dram-sipping fellows retreat,
> But your beer-drinking Britons can never be beat.

The song was inserted into Lewis Theobald's popular pantomime *Harlequin Mercury* in 1757. Another work of Garrick, "Hearts of Oak," became a popular song throughout England and the author, in acknowledging James Boswell's account of singing it for his Corsican hosts, admitted to the Scotsman, with understandable satisfaction: ". . . tho I have heard it sung from North to South & East to West in England, yet I never dreamt that it would reach Corsica."[4]

As patriotic ideals drew Garrick's exalted sentiments, so personal relationships produced some of his most pointed statements. In the case of Kitty Clive, one of his favorite actresses, who had remarked that she was as well qualified to wear breeches as Garrick was to play Ranger in Hoadly's *The Suspicious Husband*, Garrick was playful:

> Dear Kate, it is vanity both us bewitches,
>      Since I must the truth on't reveal,
> For when I *mount the ladder,* and *you* wear the *breeches,*
>      We shew—what *we ought to conceal.*

But for Dr. John Hill, the physician-playwright who was one of Garrick's prime antagonists, he wrote with marked acerbity upon the first performance of the doctor's farce, *The Rout:*

> For physic and farces,
> His equal there scarce is;
> His farces are physic,
> His physic a farce is.

Garrick had learned not only how to provide the explosive comment in a short poem such as the epigram, but also how to use the poetic form as an instrument of sustained attack. Thaddeus Fitzpatrick, a disappointed playwright and critic, and the self-appointed leader of a group of young men who called themselves "The Town," had launched a venomous attack upon Garrick through a series of letters, issued almost weekly, which were published in Arthur Murphy's *Craftsman or Gray's-Inn Journal* over the signature "X.Y.Z." Though Fitzpatrick was unhappy with Garrick's managerial policies, particularly his attempt to rid Drury Lane of the practice of admitting patrons after the third act for half of the admission charge, he focused his attack more personally upon Garrick's acting. The letters were collected and reprinted in 1760, together with Fitzpatrick's essay, "An Inquiry into the Real Merit of a Certain Popular Performer."

In contrast to the hammering approach of his attacker, Garrick responded with apparent lightness in *The Fribbleriad,* which he published anonymously in 1761. Alluding to the despicable Fribble of his own farce, *Miss in Her Teens* (1747), he cleverly decimates his enemy by questioning his sexual identity:

> So smiling, smirking, soft in feature,
> You'd swear it was the gentlest creature—
> But touch its pride, the *lady-fellow,*

> From sickly pale, turns deadly yellow—
> *Male, female,* vanish—fiends appear—
> And all is malice, rage, and fear!

Garrick depicts a meeting of the Fribbles "for plotting and intriguing" at which Fitzgig is voted into leadership to pursue the Fribbles' objective: to attack Garrick because the playwright had satirized them in *Miss in Her Teens*. Fitzgig dictates the Fribbles' course of attack:

> With this [his pen], while living, I'll dissect him;
> Create his errors, then detect 'em;
> Swell tiny faults to monstrous size!
> Then point them out to purblind eyes,
> ............................................
> . . . . His very merit I'll pervert,
> And swear the ore is sand and dirt.

Thus Garrick emerges as the hero of the poem, as the meeting, it is suggested, explains the reason for the rancor of the "X.Y.Z." attacks on him. Garrick is asked, at the end of the poem: "Can you their rage with justice blame?/ To you they owe their public shame." Though Garrick the poet lacks the rapier wit of the Augustan satirist, his dramatist's gift for creating situation and his disdainful view of the Fribbles, which renders them ludicrous though not dangerous, created an effective poetic response to his antagonists.[5]

In "The Sick Monkey," published in 1765, Garrick used his poetic abilities in order to solidify his position as playwright and actor before returning to Drury Lane following his eighteen-month tour of the Continent. He had left London in 1763, exhausted physically and emotionally by the demands of writing, managing, and acting, and further weakened by the disturbances caused by the half-price riots engineered by Fitzpatrick. In 1765, still unable to decide whether he should return to immerse himself fully in the life of Drury Lane, Garrick wrote "The Sick Monkey, a Fable," in Paris and sent it to George Colman, who was, with George Garrick, managing Drury Lane in Garrick's absence. Garrrick asked him to publish it in a London newspaper at the time of his return to that city. The poem suggests that small-minded criticism is absolutely predictable.

> And will not fools
> Thy mock'ry ridicules,

> From CHALKSTONE'S Lord to dainty FRIBBLE,
>     Rave, chatter, write,
> In various ways display their spite?

The fable itself is simple: Pug, the monkey-prodigy, languishes because of the loss of curl in his tail. His doctor advises him to take a vacation, which he does and returns "A greater monkey than before." In the last stanza Garrick is told baldly to observe the same prescription as the monkey did when he comes upon violent criticism: "Keep the poison from your Head,/ And clap it to your TAIL." The poem served to announce Garrick's return to London and allowed him to assess the climate of cordiality to which he would return.

## "Ode upon Dedicating a Building to Shakespeare"

When Garrick planned the Shakespeare Jubilee of 1769, he envisioned the Ode as the central event. He composed the poem, had Dr. Arne set it to music, and arranged for a chorus of one hundred to accompany him in the recitation. Although most of the events were enacted in the midst of three days of heavy English downpour, the rains abated sufficiently for Garrick to recite the ode before two thousand spectators at noon on September 7, 1769. The enthralled audience was delighted to hear Garrick lead an antiphonal ode, rather than simply recite a lengthy poem. Shakespeare is hailed as a demigod, "the god of our idolatry," by the speaker. Garrick's sound musical sense, apparent in his writing of musical plays, is evident.

The language used in the choruses is dignified and exalted:

> Swell the choral song,
> Roll the tide of harmony along,
>     Let Rapture sweep the strings,
>     Fame expand her wings,
> With her trumpet-tongues proclaim
> The lov'd, rever'd immortal name,
> Shakespeare! Shakespeare! Shakespeare!

This language contrasts dramatically with that of the interpolated airs, where the words are simple and sweet:

> Sweetest bard that ever sung,
> *Nature's* glory, *Fancy's* child,

> Never sure did witching tongue
> Warble forth such wood-notes wild.

In dignified language the speaker explains the appropriateness of homage to Shakespeare: "Nature had form'd him on her noblest plan,/ And to that genius join'd the feeling man." The poem ends on a reverential note, as the speaker addresses his listeners with the searching question:

> Can *British* gratitude delay,
>     To him the glory of this isle,
>         To give the festive day
> The song, the statue, and devoted pile?
> To him, the first of poets, best of men?
> "We ne'er shall look upon his like again!"

Arne's score appropriately enhanced Garrick's poetry, creating an ode that successfully captured the essence of the poetic form and emerged, as Garrick had hoped, as the highlight of the Shakespeare Jubilee. The Ode was so popular, in fact, that Garrick recited it several times the following year during the course of the regular season at Drury Lane.

## Poems Not Related to Theater

As an eighteenth-century gentleman who expressed himself in verse with ease and facility, Garrick wrote numerous poems that dealt with life beyond the theater. Some were poems that he turned out as a public figure, drawn as he was into the orbit of public life; others were written to close friends, dealing with common situations. Both the poems written as a public figure and those written as a private person demonstrate Garrick's concern for others, his consistency of view, and his expertise in selecting the correct word and felicitous phrase. Garrick wrote the "Epitaph on William Hogarth" to be inscribed on his tomb, with some formality, lauding the painter's contribution to art:

> Farewel, great painter of mankind,
>     Who reach'd the noblest point of art;
> Whose pictur'd morals charm the mind,
>     And thro' the eye correct the heart!

But his epitaph on Claudy Philips, the musician who died in a destitute state, is kindly, personal, and gentle:

> Rest here, distress'd by poverty no more,
> Here find that calm, thou gav'st so oft before.
> Sleep, undisturb'd, within this peaceful shrine,
> 'Till angels wake thee, with a note like thine.

Garrick's verse was often uplifting and celebratory, as is his poem "On Johnson's Dictionary," in which he sees Johnson, the single lexicographer, making a greater contribution to language than the august French Academy. The same use of hyperbole for compliment is evident in the poem, "To Mr. Gray, on the Publication of his Odes in 1757," in which Garrick notes the beginning of a new age in English poetry: "Homer and Pindar are rever'd no more,/ No more the Stagyrite is law."

Garrick's stature as a public figure may be gauged by the fact that his name was often proposed as a candidate for Parliament. Receiving an inquiry on his availability from Lord Lyttelton in 1755, Garrick declined in verse, playfully noting the similarities between actor and statesman. He concluded his verse thus:

> Were it my state to quit the mimic art,
> I'd "strut and fret" no more in any part;
> No more in public scenes would I engage,
> Or wear the cap and mask on any stage.

Garrick's verses to women are often gracefully turned compliments, peopled by figures such as Phoebus, Sylvia, Arachne, Pallas, and Chloe. One of them, "Upon reading *Sir Eldred of the Bower,* by a Lady, After Lord Chesterfield's Letters," celebrates Hannah More's poem, offering it as evidence to disprove Chesterfield's contention that women have no genius. But perhaps the most successful of Garrick's poems to women is the lovely, "On GRACE," a delicate tribute to Her Royal Highness, the wife of William Augustus, Duke of Cumberland:

> But where it is,—all hearts agree:
> 'Tis there, when easy in its state,
> The mind is elegantly great;
> Where looks give speech to ev'ry feature,
> The sweetest eloquence of nature.

Besides paying a graceful compliment, Garrick sometimes used his verse to make pointed and incisive statements, as in his lines, "On Lord Warwick's Invitation," in which the poet expresses his chagrin after being dismissed by Warwick, with whom he had planned to spend the week at His Lordship's castle. Garrick wrote another poem in the same vein upon hearing that a certain lord had paid the very substantial sum of £1,000 for a house:

> So many thousands for a house
> For you, of all the world, lord Mouse!
> A little house would best accord
> With you, my very little lord!
> And then exactly match'd would be
> Your house and hospitality.

But in the poems he wrote to his friends, Garrick's verse was direct, personal, and generous. In complimenting George Colman on his translation of Terence, Garrick concludes: "Joy to myself! for all the fame/ Which ever shall attend thy name,/ I feel as half my own." The same note of sincerity is evident in a poem written on the back of his picture which Garrick sent to a friend, "a Gentleman of the University of Oxford,"

> The mimic form on t 'other side,
> That you accepted is my pride;
> Resembles one so prompt to change,
> Through ev'ry mortal whim to range,
> You'd swear the lute so like the case,
> The mind as various as the face.
> Yet to his friends be this his fame,
> His heart's eternally the same.

## Garrick's Achievement as Poet

Compared to his contributions to the theater, Garrick's accomplishments as poet appear minor and, consequently, have generally received little attention from his biographers and critics. Yet the significance of the poetry is undeniable for those who wish to gain an insight into the mind and art of the playwright, actor, and manager. The great bulk of his poetry deals with the life of the theater and provides a perspective on the subject not available in any other form.

The nontheatrical poetry gives us comparable insight into Garrick the man.

Because prologues and epilogues were written to be delivered to a playhouse audience, they were subject to the same vagaries of audience favor and disfavor as were the plays. In framing the plays, therefore, they attempted to capture the attention of the audience and to entice them into the psychological world of the play. Often this included discussing and disposing of significant events in the theatrical milieu, commenting on the manners of the town and the audience, and indicating the importance of the work to be presented. Thus, the prologues and epilogues may be read as a miniature chronicle of the theatrical events of the period. The 114 songs that Garrick wrote, mostly for performance within the plays, indicate the increasingly musical flavor of the theater as the century progressed. And the longer theatrical poems, such as "The Fribbleriad," "The Sick Monkey," and "An Ode Upon Dedicating a Building to Shakespeare," though not written for performance within plays, supply many details in the larger context of the eighteenth-century theatrical world. Esthetically, many of the poems and songs are noteworthy, exploiting the literary gift Garrick had put to use in his plays: the careful choice of language, the flair for the well-turned phrase, and the good-humored approach to life.

As the theatrical poems provide an informal record of theatrical events, so the nontheatrical poems provide a slender history of the social life of the period. These poems give evidence of the uses of occasional verse in the life of an eighteenth-century gentleman, from formal tributes to the dead, to graceful compliments to female friends, to the use of poems as bread-and-butter thank-you notes.[6] Some contain exalted sentiments and were written for important moments; others are saturated in everyday affairs and record such minutiae as social embarrassments. Some few poems, intended for his intimate friends, provide additional insight into Garrick the man who, though often attacked by his antagonists, emerges as warm, direct, and generous in feeling.

Written with clarity and grace, Garrick's poetry is a large and diversified body of work. Though none of it can claim to be original in form, the sentiments are particularized and timeless images are given timely application.

# Chapter Seven
# Conclusion

Garrick's poetry is one more instance of his signature upon his time, amplifying and reinforcing his substantial contributions to literary and theatrical life. Universally acknowledged as the exponent of a new, more natural style of acting that revolutionized theatrical practice, Garrick was respected as indisputably the finest actor of his day. His intellectualized appreciation of the art of acting and his psychological insights into the characters he portrayed informed his playwright's pen. Garrick, whose sensibilities were thus honed by the finely tuned instincts of the actor, enjoyed a playwriting career of thirty-five years.

During that time he produced clever comedies of manners, gently satiric plays, and laugh-provoking farces. Most of them were sturdy theater pieces built upon well-delineated characterizations and fast-moving plots. From these works came Fribble and Timothy Sharp, Lord Chalkstone and Lord Ogleby, characters who have never been duplicated upon the English stage. Garrick recognized, too, that music could add a dimension to drama not attainable by words alone and he wrote plays in which music often advanced the plot, transported the audience to a land of fantasy, celebrated topics of popular interest, and heightened and focused his comedy.

And while Garrick manufactured his own comic creations, he was also painstakingly attempting to restore and adapt the works of other playwrights. Long a student of Shakespeare, he felt compelled to extricate the pure poetry of his plays from the weight of the Restoration and early eighteenth-century adaptations in which many were encased. Directed by the instincts of the actor, he attempted to restore the original texts of the great Shakespearean plays: *King Lear, Antony and Cleopatra, Cymbeline, Hamlet, Macbeth, Romeo and Juliet,* and *The Tempest.* Often he was able to bring genuine Shakespearean verse to the playhouse for the first time since Shakespeare's own day; at other times his efforts were circumscribed by the custom-bound expectations of his audience, so that his success was only partial. But all his attempts—those that succeeded and those that failed to restore the full Shakespearean text—left his audiences closer to experiencing Shakespeare than they would have been otherwise.

His other adaptations also bore the imprint of his efforts to bring to his audiences the best theatrical experiences available from other times and other cultures. Thus he selected significant and actable plays from English Renaissance drama, English Restoration drama, and contemporary French and English drama and, turning his sharp theatrical insights upon them, wrought them into a form in which they might be appreciated by his contemporaries.

Although considerably varied, Garrick's works, informed by the experience of the actor and the aspirations of the playwright, share a number of common characteristics. To achieve the maximum impact from the theatrical situation, action was fast-paced, repartee lively, and characterization of protagonists and antagonists was not only communicated by those players, but closely supported by words and actions of ancillary characters. Further, Garrick often engaged the interest of his audience through topical references to contemporary personalities and events, and he provided them with positive, acclamatory feelings by writing artful final scenes which included most of the characters and which brought about an effective curtain.

Garrick's playwriting abilities and his theatrical acumen were informed by the writer's view that theater ought to make a positive contribution to the life of a civilized society. Thus Garrick—playwright, adapter, prologuist—always suggested to his audience, explicitly or implicitly, a code of right conduct, informed by reason and good humor. And his suggestions were made so cleverly, so amiably, and so unobtrusively that no one mistook him for a moralist.

Master playwright, renowned actor, respected theatrical manager, David Garrick was deeply immersed in eighteenth-century London life and gives us, through his plays, a delightfully good-humored view of its people, its energies, its values, and its playhouse audience.

# Notes and References

## Chapter One

1. Gilbert Walmesley to John Colson, February 5, 1737, in *The Private Correspondence of David Garrick with the Most Celebrated Persons of His Time,* ed. James Boaden (London: Henry Colburn and Richard Bentley, 1831); hereafter cited as *Garrick Correspondence.*

2. James Boswell, *Life of Johnson,* ed. G. B. Hill and L. F. Powell, 6 vols. (Oxford University Press, 1934–50), 1:80–81; hereafter cited as Boswell's *Johnson.*

3. March 2, 1737, *Garrick Correspondence.*

4. Boswell's *Johnson* 3:387.

5. George Winchester Stone, Jr., and George M. Kahrl, *David Garrick: a Critical Biography* (Carbondale, Ill., 1979), p. 282.

6. William Windham, *The Diary of the Right Hon. William Windham, 1784–1810,* ed. Mrs. Henry Baring (London: 1810), p. 361.

7. See Stone and Kahrl, *David Garrick,* pp. 52–96.

8. Philip H. Highfill, Jr., Kalman A. Burnim, and Edward A. Langhans, *A Biographical Dictionary of Actors, Actresses, Musicians, Dancers, Managers & Other Stage Personnel in London, 1660–1800.* (Carbondale, Ill., 1973– ), 6:112–16.

9. See Stone and Kahrl, *David Garrick,* pp. 126–31; 596–600.

10. Highfill et al., *Biographical Dictionary* 6:65.

11. Boswell's *Johnson* 2:464.

## Chapter Two

1. *British Dramatists from Dryden to Sheridan,* ed. George H. Nettleton and Arthur E. Case, rev. George Winchester Stone, Jr. (Carbondale, Ill., 1969), p. 626.

2. *Letters of David Garrick,* ed. David M. Little and George M. Kahrl (London, 1963), 2:535; hereafter cited as *Garrick Letters.*

3. See Frederick Bergmann, "David Garrick and *The Clandestine Marriage,*" *PMLA* 67 (1952):148–62.

4. All scene and line references to Garrick's plays are drawn from *The Plays of David Garrick,* ed. Harry William Pedicord and Frederick Louis Bergmann (Carbondale, Ill., 1980–82). In the case of one-act plays, only two numbers are given, for scene and line. References are cited within the text in parentheses. Cited in notes as *Garrick Plays.*

5. Alan D. Guest, "Charles Adams and John Gilbert Cooper," *Theatre Notebook* 11 (1957):138.

6. The diaries of Richard Cross and William Hopkins are printed passim in *The London Stage 1660–1800,* part 4, ed. George Winchester Stone, Jr., 3 vols. (Carbondale, Ill., Southern Illinois University Press, 1962). Entries are under their appropriate dates in *The London Stage,* and references will be made in the text by date.

7. Arthur Murphy, *The Life of David Garrick* (London: 1801; reprint, New York, 1969), 1:308.

8. *Garrick Letters* 1:33–34.

9. Peter Motteux, *The Novelty: Every Act a Play* (London: Rich. Parker and Peter Buck, 1697).

10. For a full discussion of Jonson's popularity in this period, see Robert Gale Noyes, *Ben Jonson on the English Stage 1660–1776* (Cambridge, Mass., 1935; reprint, New York: Benjamin Blom, 1966).

11. Murphy, *Life* 1:117–18. For another description of Woodward as Captain Flash, see John Genest, *Some Account of the English Stage. . . 1660–1830* (Bath, 1832; reprint, New York, n.d.), 4:213–14.

12. Genest, *English Stage* 4:213.

13. Murphy, *Life* 1:297–98.

14. In 1762, in Cock Lane, Smithfield, certain knockings were heard which were thought to proceed from the ghost of Fanny Kent, who died suddenly, and who was thought to have been murdered. All London seemed titillated by the story. Finally, it was discovered that the knockings were produced by a twelve-year-old girl who rapped on a board.

15. Murphy, *Life* 1:367.

16. *Garrick Letters* 2:917.

17. Ibid., p. 782.

18. William Hopkins, prompter at Drury Lane, records in his Diary for March 18, 1775, that the play was "Written 15 or 16 years ago. Mr. Garrick out of friendship for Mr. King gave it him to get up for his Benefit."

19. Elizabeth P. Stein, *David Garrick, Dramatist* (New York: 1938; reprint, New York, 1967), p. 64.

20. Ibid., p. 197.

21. *Garrick Letters* 1:412.

22. Ibid., 2:430.

23. Bergmann, *"Clandestine Marriage,"* pp. 148–62.

24. For a full discussion of the genesis of the play, see "Commentary and Notes," *Garrick Plays* 1:413–20.

25. Thomas Davies, *Memoirs of the Life of David Garrick, Esq.* (London, 1808), 2:102–3.

26. *Garrick Plays* 1:419.

27. *Garrick Letters* 2:690.

## Chapter Three

1. George C. D. Odell, *Shakespeare from Betterton to Irving*, (New York, 1920; reprint, New York, 1966), 1:359.

2. For a discussion of Garrick's influence on Guadagni's career, see Charles Burney, *A General History of Music* (London, 1789; reprint, New York, 1957), 2:875.

3. Tate Wilkinson, *Memoirs of His Own Life* (York, Wilson, Spence, and Mawman, 1790), 4:202.

4. Odell, *Shakespeare* 1:32.

5. Roger Fiske, *English Theatre Music in the Eighteenth Century* (London, 1973), p. 245.

6. Wilkinson, *Memoirs* 4:213.

7. Murphy, *Life* 2:302–3.

8. Theophilus Cibber, *Two Dissertations Upon the Theatres* (London, 1756), "First Dissertation," p. 36.

9. Davies, *Memoirs* 1:129–30.

10. Parallels between *Harlequin's Invasion* and *Harlequin Student* are noted in *Garrick Plays* 1:406, and Fiske, *English Theatre Music*, p. 236.

11. Henry Angelo, *Reminiscences of Henry Angelo*, 2 vols. (London, 1828–30), 1:10–15.

12. See Professor Knapp's discussion of the music for *The Enchanter* in "English Theatrical Music in Garrick's Time: *The Enchanter* (1760) and May Day (1775)" in *The Stage and the Page*, ed. George Winchester Stone, Jr. (Berkeley, 1981), pp. 116–35.

13. Horace Walpole to the Reverend William Cole, *Letters*, ed. Mrs. Paget Toynbee, 16 vols. (London, 1903), 8:141.

14. See especially Stein, *David Garrick*, pp. 120–26, 156.

15. *The London Stage*, part 4, 1208.

16. Ibid., part 5, 1416.

17. Angelo, *Reminiscences* 2:326–7.

18. Walpole, *Letters* 8:398.

19. See Phyllis T. Dircks, "Garrick's Fail-Safe Musical Venture: *A Peep Behind the Curtain*, an English Burletta" in *The Stage and the Page*, pp. 136–47, for a discussion of the backgrounds of the burletta. See also Kane O'Hara, *Midas: an English Burletta*, Introduction by P. T. Dircks, Augustan Reprint Society Publication, no. 167 (Los Angeles, William Andrews Clark Memorial Library, 1974), pp. i–xi.

20. See Stoddard Lincoln, "Barthelemon's Setting of Garrick's *Orpheus*," in *The Stage and the Page*, pp. 148–59.

21. Knapp, "English Theatrical Music," p. 135.

22. The subject is fully treated in Christian Deelman, *The Great Shakespeare Jubilee* (New York, 1964); Martha Winburn England, *Garrick's Jubilee*

(Columbus, Ohio, 1964); and Johanne Stochholm, *Garrick's Folly*, (New York, 1964).

23. *Garrick Letters* 2:675–77.

24. John O'Keeffe, *Recollections of the Life of John O'Keeffe*, 2 vols. (London, 1826), 1:150.

25. See reviews in *Town and Country Magazine* (September 1775) and *Westminster Magazine* (September 1775).

*Chapter Four*

1. Hazelton Spencer, *Shakespeare Improved* (Cambridge, Mass., 1927; reprint, New York, 1963), p. 158.

2. George Winchester Stone, Jr., "Garrick's Handling of *Macbeth*," *Studies in Philology* 38 (October 1941): 622.

3. Jean Georges Noverre, *Letters on Dancing and Ballets*, trans. C. W. Beaumont (London, 1830), pp. 84–85.

4. John Downes, *Roscius Anglicanus* (London, 1708), ed. Montague Summers, (London: 1929; reprint, New York: Benjamin Blom, 1968), p. 22.

5. Count Frederick Kielmansegge, *Diary of a Journey to England 1761–62*, trans. Countess Kielmansegge (London: Longmans & Co., 1902), pp. 221–22.

6. Francis Gentleman, *The Dramatic Censor* (London, 1770; reprint, New York, 1972), 1:185.

7. Ibid., p. 187.

8. Murphy, *Life* 1:152–53.

9. See *Spectator* #40 in which Addison claims that, in Tate's version, *Lear* "has lost half its beauty." In 1747, in the *Examen of the New Comedy call'd the Suspicious Husband*, to which he added a "Word of Advice to Mr. Garrick," Samuel Foote urged Garrick to produce the play "by giving us *Lear* in the original, fool and all."

10. George Winchester Stone, Jr., "Garrick's Production of *King Lear*," *Studies in Philology* 45 (January 1948):91.

11. *Garrick Letters* 2:682–83.

12. Thomas Davies, *Dramatic Miscellanies* (Dublin, 1784; reprint, New York, 1971), 2:172.

13. Stone, *Lear*, p. 94.

14. Stone and Kahrl, *David Garrick*, p. 265.

15. Representative later reactions may be found in Genest, 4:475 and Odell, 1:377.

16. George Winchester Stone, Jr., "Shakespeare's *Tempest* at Drury Lane," *Shakespeare Quarterly*, 7 (Winter 1956):5.

17. Genest, *English Stage* 4:564.

18. Odell, *Shakespeare* 1:8–9.

19. *Garrick Letters* 3:1095.

20. James Boaden, *Memoirs of the Life of John Philip Kemble*, 2 vols. (London, 1825; reprint, New York, Benjamin Blom, 1969), 1:111–12.

21. Stone and Kahrl, *David Garrick*, p. 273.

22. Davies, *Dramatic Miscellanies* 3:86–87.

23. Stone and Kahrl, *David Garrick*, p. 271.

24. See Boaden, *Kemble* 1:112; Odell, *Shakespeare* 1:385–90; Frank A. Hedgcock, *David Garrick and His French Friends* (London, 1912; reprint, New York, 1969), pp. 77–79.

25. *London Chronicle*, December 17–19, 1772; *Westminster Magazine* 1 (1773):34; *Macaroni and Theatrical Magazine*, December, 1772, p. 119.

26. *Garrick Letters* 2:841–42.

*Chapter Five*

1. Stone and Kahrl, *David Garrick*, p. 282.

2. Gerard Langbaine, *An Account of the English Dramatic Poets* (Oxford, 1691), p. 290; Noyes, *Ben Jonson*, pp. 246–50.

3. Murphy, *Life* 1:205–6.

4. Ibid., 207–8.

5. *Some Unpublished Correspondence of David Garrick*, ed. G. P. Baker (Boston, Houghton Mifflin, 1907), p. 80.

6. Davies, *Dramatic Miscellanies* 2:42.

7. Thomas Wilkes, *A General View of the Stage* (London, 1759), pp. 258–59.

8. Walpole, *Letters* 10:370.

9. Felix Schelling, *English Drama* (London: J. M. Dent & Sons, and New York: E. P. Dutton, 1914), p. 208.

10. *The Theatrical Review* (London, 1758), pp. 69–70.

11. Genest, *English Stage* 4:512–13.

12. Georg Christoph Lichtenberg, *Lichtenberg's Visits to England*, translated and annotated by Margaret L. Mare and W. H. Quarrell (Oxford, 1938; reprint, New York, 1969), pp. 18–19.

13. Gentleman, *Dramatic Censor* 2:470.

14. The prompt copy is located at the Folger Shakespeare Library. See *Garrick Plays* 6:383–84 for particulars.

15. *Garrick Plays* 6:388–89.

16. Stone and Kahrl, *David Garrick*, p. 269.

17. Thomas Campbell, *Dr. Campbell's Diary of a Visit to England in 1775,* ed. James L. Clifford (Cambridge: University Press, 1947), p. 47.

18. Joseph Cradock, *Literary and Miscellaneous Memoirs*, 4 vols. (London, 1826–8), 1:206.

*Chapter Six*

1. "Preface," *The Poetical Works of David Garrick, Esq.*, 2 vols. (London, 1785), pp. iii–iv.

2. Stone and Kahrl, *David Garrick*, pp. 387–88.

3. Ibid., p. 398.

4. *Garrick Letters* 2:600–601.

5. See Genest, *English Stage* 5:14–17 for detailed account.

6. See *Garrick Letters* 2:464–65, 687–88, 697–98, 704–5, 774–75, 3:963–64, 1280.

# Selected Bibliography

## PRIMARY SOURCES

*The Diary of David Garrick: Being a record of his memorable trip to Paris in 1751.* Edited by Ryllis Clair Alexander. Oxford: Oxford University Press, 1929: Reprint. New York: Benjamin Blom, 1971.

*An Essay On Acting: in which will be consider'd the mimical behaviour of a certain fashionable faulty actor.* London: W. Bickerton, 1744.

*The Letters of David Garrick.* 3 vols. Edited by David M. Little and George M. Kahrl, with associate editor Phoebe deK. Wilson. London: Oxford University Press, 1963.

*The Plays of David Garrick.* 7 vols. Edited by Harry William Pedicord and Frederick Louis Bergmann. Carbondale: Southern Illinois University Press, 1980–82.

*The Poetical Works of David Garrick.* 2 vols. London: George Kearsley, 1785. Reprint. New York: Benjamin Blom, 1968.

## SECONDARY SOURCES

### 1. Books

Bevis, Richard. *The Laughing Tradition: Stage Comedy in Garrick's Day.* Athens, Ga.: University of Georgia Press, 1980. Maintains viability of laughing comedy throughout Garrick era, particularly in afterpieces.

Boswell, James. *Life of Johnson.* 6 vols. Edited by G. B. Hill and L. F. Powell. Oxford: Oxford University Press, 1934–50. Documents Garrick's relationship with Samuel Johnson.

Burney, Charles. *A General History of Music From the Earliest Ages to the Present Period.* 2 vols. London: Constable & Company, 1789. Reprint. New York: Dover Publications, 1957. Authoritative account of musical performances on London stage of Garrick's time.

Burnim, Kalman. *David Garrick, Director.* Pittsburgh: University of Pittsburgh Press, 1961. Reprint. Carbondale: Southern Illinois University Press, 1973. Study of Garrick's directing techniques and practices and their application to his alterations of *Macbeth, Romeo and Juliet, King Lear, Hamlet,* and *The Provok'd Wife.*

Davies, Thomas. *Dramatic Miscellanies.* 3 vols. Dublin: S. Price et al., 1784. Reprint. New York: Benjamin Blom, 1971. Anecdotal account of dramatic representation of selected Shakespearean plays, as well as those of Jonson, Dryden, Otway, Buckingham, Congreve, and Cibber. Includes information on actors and actresses.

————— . *Memoirs of the Life of David Garrick*. 2 vols. London: Longman, Hurst, Rees & Orme, 1808. Reprint. New York: Benjamin Blom, 1969. Anecdotal account of Garrick's life and career. Contains contributions of Samuel Johnson.

Deelman, Christian. *The Great Shakespeare Jubilee*. New York: Viking Press, 1964. Thorough account of preparations for and celebration of Garrick's Shakespeare Jubilee in 1769.

Dircks, Richard. *Richard Cumberland*. Boston: Twayne Publishers, 1976. Documents Garrick's contribution to Cumberland as dramatist.

England, Martha Winburn. *Garrick's Jubilee*. Columbus, Ohio: Ohio State University Press, 1964. Account of Shakespeare Jubilee of 1769, with valuable section on European reactions.

Fiske, Roger. *English Theatre Music in the Eighteenth Century*. London: Oxford University Press, 1973. Encyclopedic study of theatrical music which credits Garrick with intelligent interest in musical productions.

Fitzgerald, Percy. *The Life of David Garrick*. London: Simpkin, Marshall, Hamilton, Kent & Co., 1899. Anecdotal account attempting to cover all phases of Garrick's life.

Genest, John. *Some Account of the English Stage from the Restoration in 1660 to 1830*. 10 vols. Bath: H. E. Carrington, 1832. Though superseded by *The London Stage 1660–1800*, it nevertheless contains valuable accounts of Garrick's plays, both in plot and performance.

Gentleman, Francis. *The Dramatic Censor; or Critical Companion*. 2 vols. London: J. Bell & C. Etherington, 1770. Reprint. New York: Benjamin Blom, 1972. An evaluation of the most significant plays in the eighteenth-century repertory, with discussions of performances by Garrick and his contemporaries.

Hedgcock, Frank A. *A Cosmopolitan Actor: David Garrick and His French Friends*. London: Stanley Paul & Co., 1912. Reprint. New York: Benjamin Blom, 1969. Debunking account which admits only to Garrick's excellence as an actor.

Highfill, Philip H., Jr., Kalman A. Burnim, and Edward A. Langhans. *A Biographical Dictionary of Actors, Actresses, Musicians, Dancers, Managers, and Other Stage Personnel in London, 1660–1800*. 6 vols. Carbondale: Southern Illinois University Press, 1973–. Authoritative and detailed accounts of all theater personnel.

Hughes, Leo. *A Century of English Farce*. Princeton: Princeton University Press, 1956 Reprint. Westport, Conn.: Greenwood Press, 1979. Locates Garrick's farces within the tradition, emphasizing their theatricality.

Hume, Robert D., ed. *The London Theatre World 1660–1800*. Carbondale: Southern Illinois University Press, 1980. Twelve essays surveying theatrical conditions, with rich sections on the repertory and performers.

Knight, Joseph. *David Garrick*. London: Kegan Paul, Trench, Trubner & Co., 1894. Generally negative portrait of man and dramatist.

Lichtenberg, Georg Christoph. *Lichtenberg's Visits to England*. Translated and annotated by Margaret L. Mare and W. H. Quarrell. Oxford: Oxford University Press, 1938. Reprint. New York: Benjamin Blom, 1969. Contains extremely detailed accounts of Garrick on stage as perceived by visiting German professor.

Murphy, Arthur. *The Gray's Inn Journal*. London: W. Faden & J. Bouquet, 1753–54. Contemporary dramatic criticism, especially of Shakespearean plays.

———. *Life of David Garrick*. 2 vols. London: J. Wright, 1801. Reprint. New York: Benjamin Blom, 1969. Sympathetic, anecdotal account of Garrick.

Nettleton, George H., Arthur E. Case, and George Winchester Stone, Jr. *British Dramatists from Dryden to Sheridan*. Carbondale: Southern Illinois University Press, 1969. Generous anthology with a good discussion of the afterpiece as "a touchstone of eighteenth-century popular taste."

Nicoll, Allardyce. *The Garrick Stage: Theatres and Audience in the Eighteenth Century*. Athens, Ga.: University of Georgia Press, 1980. Study of conditions of physical theater.

———. *A History of Early Eighteenth Century Drama 1700–1750*. Cambridge: Cambridge University Press, 1969. Overview of dramatic activity in period.

———. *A History of Late Eighteenth Century Drama 1750–1800*. Cambridge: Cambridge University Press, 1969. Overview of dramatic activity in period.

Noyes, Robert Gale. *Ben Jonson on the English Stage 1660–1776*. Cambridge, Mass.: Harvard University Press, 1935. Reprint. New York: Benjamin Blom, 1966. Detailed study of influence of Jonson on Garrick and his contemporaries.

Odell, George C. D. *Shakespeare from Betterton to Irving*. 2 vols. New York: Charles Scribner's Sons, 1920. Reprint. New York, Dover Publications, 1966. Useful background information on Shakespearean productions.

O'Hara, Kane. *Midas: an English Burletta*. "Introduction" by P. T. Dircks. Los Angeles: William Andrews Clark Memorial Library, 1974. Augustan Reprint Society Publication no. 167. Popular burletta which influenced Garrick in his writing *A Peep Behind the Curtain*.

Parsons, Mrs. Clement. *Garrick and His Circle*. London: 1906. Reprint. New York: Benjamin Blom, 1969. Unsympathetic account focusing on personality rather than accomplishments.

Pedicord, Harry William. *The Theatrical Public in the Time of Garrick*. New York: 1954. Reprint. Carbondale: Southern Illinois University Press, 1966. Pioneer study of Garrick's audience.

Price, Cecil. *Theatre in the Age of Garrick.* Totowa, N.J.: Rowman & Little-
field, 1973. Useful survey of the state of theatrical art.

Spencer, Hazelton. *Shakespeare Improved.* Cambridge, Mass.: Harvard University Press, 1927. Reprint. New York: Frederick Ungar Publishing
Co., 1963. Seminal discussion of Shakespearean adaptations which
were popular until Garrick's time.

Stein, Elizabeth P. *David Garrick, Dramatist.* New York, 1938. Reprint.
New York: Benjamin Blom, 1967. Detailed consideration of Garrick's
farces, satires, and musical works.

Stochholm, Johanne M. *Garrick's Folly.* New York: Barnes & Noble,
1964. Reconstruction of events of Shakespeare Jubilee, 1769.

Stone, George Winchester, Jr., ed. *The Stage and the Page: London's "Whole
Show" in the Eighteenth Century Theatre.* Berkeley: University of Califor-
nia Press, 1981. Twelve essays exploring interrelationship of dramatic
text and theatrical production.

————, and George M. Kahrl. *David Garrick: A Critical Biography.* Carbondale: Southern Illinois University Press, 1979. Comprehensive,
fully authoritative study of Garrick as manager, dramatist, producer,
actor, and private man.

Toynbee, Mrs. Paget, ed. *The Letters of Horace Walpole,* 16 vols. Oxford:
Oxford University Press, 1903–5. Lively contemporary comments on
the theatrical milieu by a leading member of Garrick's society.

Van Lennep, William, Emmet L. Avery, Arthur H. Scouten, George
Winchester Stone, Jr., and Charles Beecher Hogan. *The London
Stage 1660–1800.* 11 vols. Carbondale: Southern Illinois University
Press, 1960–68. Standardized calendar of theatrical productions con-
taining comprehensive introductions to each of five periods: 1660–
1700; 1700–1729; 1729–1747; 1747–1776; 1776–1800.

2. Articles

Bergmann, Frederick L. "David Garrick and *The Clandestine Marriage.*"
*PMLA* 67 (March 1952):148–62. Demonstration, based on new manuscript evidence, that Garrick wrote most significant portions of play.

————. "Garrick's *Zara.*" *PMLA* 74 (June 1959):225–32. Argues that
Garrick revised Hill's translation; thus work should be added to Garrick canon.

Dircks, P. T. "The Eighteenth-Century Burletta: Problems of Research."
*Restoration and Eighteenth-Century Theatre Research* 10 (November 1971):44–
52. Bibliographic evidence of the confusion of terms attached to type
of musical play that interested Garrick.

Dircks, Richard. "Garrick and Gentleman: Two Interpretations of Abel
Drugger." *Restoration and Eighteenth-Century Theatre Research* 7 (November 1968):48–55. Analysis of alterations in the role of Jonson's Abel
Drugger made by Garrick in his alteration and by Gentleman in a
prose farce, *The Tobacconist.*

Gottesman, Lillian. "Garrick's *Institution of the Garter.*" *Restoration and Eighteenth-Century Theatre Research* 6 (November 1967):37–43. Discussion of play based on Larpent manuscript and printed edition of songs only.

———. "Garrick's *Lilliput.*" *Restoration and Eighteenth-Century Theatre Research* 11 (November 1972):34–37. Discussion of confrontation episode in play.

Scouten, Arthur H. "Shakespeare's Plays in the Theatrical Repertoire when Garrick Came to London." *University of Texas Studies in English.* 24 (1944):257–68. Well-documented account.

Stone, George Winchester, Jr., "A Century of *Cymbeline*; or Garrick's Magic Touch." *Philological Quarterly* 54 (Winter 1975):138–52. This and the following articles by Professor Stone provide detailed discussions of Garrick's Shakespearean alterations.

———. "David Garrick's Significance in the History of Shakespearean Criticism." *PMLA* 65 (March 1950):183–97.

———. "Garrick and an Unknown Operatic Version of *Love's Labours Lost.*" *Review of English Studies* 15 (July 1939):323–28.

———. "Garrick's Handling of *Macbeth.*" *Studies in Philology* 38 (October 1941):609–28.

———. "Garrick's Long-Lost Alteration of *Hamlet.*" *PMLA* 49 (September 1934):890–921.

———. "Garrick's Presentation of *Antony and Cleopatra.*" *Review of English Studies* 13 (January 1937):20–38.

———. "Garrick's Production of *King Lear*: A Study in the Temper of the Eighteenth-Century Mind." *Studies in Philology* 45 (January 1948):89–103.

———. "*A Midsummer Night's Dream* in the Hands of Garrick and Colman." *PMLA* 54 (June 1939):467–82.

———. "Shakespeare's *Tempest* at Drury Lane During Garrick's Management." *Shakespeare Quarterly* 7 (Winter 1956):1–7.

# Index

822.6
G241

117 418